Equipped
for
Every Good
Work

Building a Gifts-Based Church

Dan R. Dick and Barbara Miller

Reprinted 2003

Cover and book design by Nanci H. Lamar

Edited by Linda R. Whited and David Whitworth

ISBN 0-88177-352-2

Library of Congress Catalog Card No. 2001089235

DR352

Equipped for Every Good Work

Contents

WHAT IS *EQUIPPED FOR EVERY GOOD WORK?*

To be clear from the outset, what you hold in your hand is a fairly involved process for discovering the gifts and graces that God gives us to enable us to be the best church we can possibly be. By "church" we mean the people of God living faithful and fulfilling lives in the world. By "gifts and graces," we mean the God-given empowerment to make a meaningful difference in the world through the guidance of God's Spirit. By "process" we mean something that cannot be accomplished in an evening or a weekend but is an ongoing exploration of who God is calling us to be as a community of faith, today and for all the days to come. We're talking important stuff that requires a great deal of commitment.

People are hungry to know themselves and God in deep, powerful ways. There is a fundamental desire among Christians not only to live faithfully but to contribute to a purpose much greater than themselves. They turn to the church for direction and for a means to engage in critical self-examination. Often the church fails to offer processes by which this exploration may occur. *Equipped for Every Good Work*—the title is derived from instructions given in 2 Timothy 3:17—is a model for such exploration. *Equipped for Every Good Work* contains four tools for self-exploration and discovery that offer individuals insight into who they are as disciples of Jesus Christ. Even more importantly, though, it helps people discover who they are collectively as a community of faith.

Equipped for Every Good Work emerged from a program begun in 1988 by Dan Dick. The program was called the Congregational Leadership Assessment Profile (now called the Profile of Congregational Leadership—PCL). Local churches assembled key leaders from the congregation to work through three tools: a Spiritual Gifts Inventory, a Leadership/Interaction Styles Survey, and a Spirituality Type Indicator. Later, the Spirituality Type Indicator was modified to the current Spirituality Web, and the Task Type Preferences Survey was added. Though the target audience for this program is church leadership, each tool applies to anyone desiring to grow as a Christian disciple. It is important to state once again that this process was designed primarily to help individuals better understand their gifts and graces for Christian service in the world, and secondarily to help faith communities better understand the gifts and graces of the people of God who make up each local congregation. It was never intended to help local congregations identify ways to put people on committees, boards, or councils to support the program and structure of the institutional church.

The flagship tool for this process is the Spiritual Gifts Inventory. Developed from Scripture and the writings of the early Christian church fathers, this inventory describes twenty spiritual gifts and then helps people differentiate and identify their primary and secondary gifts for living as Christian disciples. Beyond discovery, the process provides the means for further exploration of the meaning of gifts, broadens the understanding of the nature and use of gifts, and offers ways to redesign the communal life of faith together in support of the gifts.

The second tool is the evaluation of Leadership/Interaction Styles (LIS). The LIS early replaced the Myers-Briggs Type (personality) Indicator in the Congregational Leadership Assessment Profile when it became clear that understanding personality types was of less value than understanding behavior. Many of the gifts that God gives pull us away from our natural comfort zones and propel us into service that does not align with our personality type. The work of David W. Merrill and Roger Reid[1] helped to move the process into the more appropriate area of behavior styles. While spiritual gifts discovery is often the motivation for congregations to enter the process, evaluation of the process consistently indicates that the LIS is the most helpful tool.

The third tool, the Spirituality Type Indicator, emerged from the writing of Urban T. Holmes.[2] It assists people in understanding more deeply both their experience of God and their approach to God. This process closely parallels the one developed by Corinne Ware,[3] but the Spirituality Type Indicator provides six Spirituality Types instead of four, and it looks at the whole life of faith rather than the worshiping life. Today, as the Spirituality Web, it no longer involves a survey format but is an interactive discussion of the six interrelated approaches to, and experiences of, God that helps a community of faith discover its diverse and textured reality.

Together, these three processes constituted the Congregational Leadership Assessment Profile during its first decade. In 1997 a fourth tool—the Task Type Preferences survey—was added to help individuals and congregations understand the kinds of work settings in which they best thrive. All four tools are the heart and soul of *Equipped for Every Good Work*, but they are, at best, a means to an end.

Ultimately, this Profile of Congregational Leadership (PCL) process is about people, not tools, and more accurately about people and their relationships to God, to self, and to the world. The church is a center for faith formation and Christian development. These tools are four ways that congregations help people grow in their self-understanding and their understanding of what it means to be the church. What follows is a look at the development of the tools and process that are *Equipped for Every Good Work* to give you a better understanding of what it does and how it can be used.

THE EVOLUTION OF A PROCESS: DAN'S JOURNEY

In 1985 a call came from a United Methodist church in Easton, Pennsylvania, requesting a workshop on spiritual gifts discovery. This was the first such request I ever received—a full decade before I began working with Barbara Miller. The only two programs on Spiritual Gifts I was aware of at that time were *Discovering Your Spiritual Gifts* by Kenneth Cain Kinghorn[4] and the *Gifts Discovery Workshop* by Herb Mather.[5] Together, these two resources offered a solid starting point for exploring spiritual gifts. I will be forever indebted to both these men for heading me down one of the most fulfilling paths in my ministry.

I went to Easton with a stack of Kinghorn's booklets and a big box of Number 2 pencils, anticipating a crowd of people—I had been told by the pastor that they were expecting around one hundred. I was nervous to be embarking on new (for me) and uncharted territory. Thirteen people showed up. I was going to spend two full days with thirteen people, leading a process that I knew virtually nothing about. I wondered how long it would take the Easton folk to catch on that I was no expert in the field.

We worked through the two-hundred-statement Kinghorn inventory—to much grumbling and fussing—and tallied the results. After identifying primary and secondary gifts, we sat in a circle and began discussing the results. Through the course of two days the mood shifted dramatically. Skeptics and critics became staunch supporters in a matter of hours. The group began to gain insight and understanding into the meaning of the gifts as we shifted from Kinghorn's data-gathering to Mather's group exploration process. As the pastor later told me, the process created a leadership "core within the core" that gained new insight into what it meant to be church.

For me, the evaluation process at the conclusion of the first retreat was most valuable. As one voice, the Easton church leaders offered three pieces of feedback.

1. The language of the inventory was too "churchy"—it felt like the inventory was designed to help the church fill leadership slots instead of help people identify their gifts.
2. It was vitally important that the materials were Bible based and supported theologically through church history and doctrine.
3. Identifying gifts is not enough; learning what to do with the gifts and how to live as gifted people is most important. The workshop (as designed at that time) focused on identifying gifts and discussing what they meant; it did nothing to develop the gifts or deploy them.

In effect, the evaluation of the first experience shaped the work that Barbara Miller and I do to this day. During the past fifteen years we have looked at dozens of spiritual gifts discovery processes. Consistently, they fail one of the three tests listed above.

The vast majority of spiritual gifts tools are designed to help the church fill leadership slots. The language of the statements casts spiritual gifts in service to the institutional church. They teach people to be good supportive church members, not how to live as gifted Christians seven days a week.

Many of the tools begin with a poor methodology. They look at today's church, they ask, "What does the church of the twenty-first century need to be effective?" they generate a list of contemporary talents needed, and then they proof-text Scripture to make the process biblical. A more sound methodology begins in Scripture. Three Pauline epistles—Romans, 1 Corinthians, and Ephesians—generate the traditional list of twenty spiritual gifts. Writings of the early church—including those of Eusebius, Clement, Tatian, Tertullian, Methodius, and others—support this list of twenty, giving rise to only one other possible spiritual gift (hospitality). Aligning today's church with the gifts revealed in Scripture has more integrity than modifying Scripture to align with today's church.

With the exception of Patricia Brown's *SpiritGifts*,[6] few processes answer the question "We've discovered what our gifts are—now what?" There is great excitement generated through the discovery process. It is similar to opening gifts on Christmas morning. However, if you receive a new, sophisticated camera for Christmas, you won't simply pick it up and start using it. You need to learn what the camera can do and how to maximize its potential. Then you need to work with it—practice—to improve your skills. The same is true with spiritual gifts. Beyond discovery there is need for learning, development, and deployment. Programs that merely identify gifts actually do a disservice to people on the faith journey by frustrating them in their efforts to know themselves more deeply. A common response I hear when I begin speaking about spiritual gifts discovery is, "Oh, we tried that. It didn't lead anywhere, so we moved on to other things."

Spiritual gifts discovery is not a program, and it is not a complete process in itself. Spiritual gifts discovery is the first step across the threshold to a lifelong journey of growth and discovery. Spiritual gifts discovery opened the way for the larger Congregational Leadership Assessment Profile process to emerge, the process that provides the basis for this book.

In 1988 the spiritual gifts work took on a new direction after I worked with an independent church in Camden, New Jersey. The small congregation pulled together two dozen leaders to engage in spiritual gifts work. Sixteen of the twenty-four church leaders possessed Evangelism as their primary gift—a rarity in most Protestant congregations. Three weeks after the event, the pastor called me to relate a problem that had developed. He said that the sixteen evangelists were at war with one another. Seven wanted to begin a street-corner ministry, handing out tracts and preaching from a platform. Another five wanted to begin a door-to-door ministry handing out congregational brochures and inviting people to church. The remaining four argued that Evangelism wasn't about making people church members, it was about the love of Jesus, and they wanted their ministry to be unrelated to the institutional church. The pastor lamented that it was better having people not know their gifts than to know them and disagree over them.

This development was a turning point in my understanding of spiritual gifts. Spiritual gifts do not exist in isolation from the fundamental nature, knowledge, and abilities of the individual. They complete the picture of whole people. Throughout the 1980's, my thinking was deeply influenced by psychologist Carl Jung and theologian Urban T. Holmes. Jung focused on personality and archetypes; Holmes on spirituality types and relationship to God. As I reflected on the breakdown of the spiritual gifts process with the Camden church, I realized that simply possessing the same gift was no guarantee that it would be used the same way. Having been certified as a trainer in the Myers-Briggs (personality) Type Indicator process, I applied what limited knowledge I had of personality types and Spirituality Types to spiritual gifts. Applying the thinking of Urban T. Holmes to the Camden situation was of great help, the Myers-Briggs process less so. Holmes identified five ways that people encounter God—through the intellect, through the emotions, through service, through mystical practice, and through radical commitment.[7] When this view was added to the spiritual gifts discovery process it offered a two-dimensional understanding of gifted people. A person who held a contemplative relationship with God would evangelize very differently from someone who lived her faith as a crusader. The five spirituality types broadened the field of spiritual gifts greatly. Each of the twenty gifts could reflect five different ways of relating to God—effectively offering a hundred different options.

Personality types added another dimension, but with fuzzier results. The problem was that people acted in unpredictable ways relative to their personality type. Intuitive people denied their intuitions to be influenced by their peer group. Introverts acted like extroverts. Perceiving people refused to act unless they received empirical proof. Deeply emotional people withdrew into critical thinking modes in the normal stresses of group interaction. The Myers-Briggs process muddied the waters instead of clearing them. Then, I encountered the work of David Merrill and Roger Reid. They, too, discovered that people often act contrary to their basic personalities. Personality analysis can help us understand why people think and feel the way they do, but it can do little to explain behavior. Merrill and Reid's work in behavioral styles added the critical third dimension to the gifts discovery process.

In the church people tend to operate predominantly from one of four behavior styles—as Directors, Dreamers, Pleasers, or Thinkers—and this predominant style will influence the way people encounter God and live from their gifts. Applying this third dimension to the work with the Camden church we realized that there were not simply sixteen Evangelists, there were Dreamer-Servant-Evangelists and Thinker-Head-Evangelists and Director-Crusader-Evangelists and Pleaser-Heart-Evangelists and many other possible combinations. In fact, there were sixteen distinctly different kinds of Evangelists. No longer did we look at a process that simply differentiated twenty kinds of gifts, we looked at one that recognized four hundred different disciple-types. Thus was born the Congregational Leadership Assessment Profile—a way of sorting through the diversity to find a common identity as leaders of a community of faith.

In 1996, two important developments occurred in the process. Examination of working styles and teams led to the development of a fourth tool—Task Types Preferences. Research showed that different people were effective in different kinds of work settings. In The United Methodist Church most work is done around committee or council tables and is not highly differentiated. Task Types divide work settings into Process, Project, Work, and Fellowship—each with a specific focus. Evaluations of the process indicate that this tool explains why certain people thrive in some settings yet are greatly ineffective in others. Added to the profile generated by spiritual gifts, spirituality types, and behavior styles, working preferences help faith communities redesign themselves for the most effective and productive service.

The second critical development in 1996 was the partnering of Barbara Miller and myself. Barbara invited me to work with her church to identify their Profile of Congregational Leadership (PCL). Through the process, the same fire that burned in my heart a decade earlier ignited in hers, and she saw a variety of ways of improving, fine-tuning, broadening, and deepening the spiritual foundation of the work. Together we have been able to raise this process to the next level. The demand for the "improved" process has been so great that we now want to make it available in its most "user-friendly" form ever.

Equipped for Every Good Work is a process of discovery and discussion of the gifts, graces, and abilities of the leadership core of a local congregation. It shifts the attention off of what we do on to who we are as called, gifted, and empowered people of God. Begun in 1988, the Profile of Congregational Leadership has been used in approximately two hundred different churches of seven denominations in settings of all shapes, sizes, locations, and racial-ethnic backgrounds. It has been used in all five jurisdictions of The United Methodist Church in thirty-one states.

RESOURCE OUTLINE

This book will follow a simple format to provide the information needed to lead the PCL process and interpret the results. Chapter 1 lays the biblical, theological, and cultural foundation for the tools and process. The spiritual gifts will be introduced and the nature of gifts will be explored. Spiritual gifts as the basis for congregational life and ministry will also be discussed.

Chapters 2 through 5 present the four tools, with detailed instructions for their use.

Examples of the four tools, frequently asked questions about the tools, anticipated results, and interpretive helps for each tool are provided. Electronic copies of handouts, overheads, and templates for all tools are available online at www.equippedforeverygoodwork.org or by mail.[8] The PCL Process Schedule in the Appendix section (pages 108-16) also provides useful information on additional presentation materials.

An intermission chapter, "A Trip to Dawson," provides a case study of a church that has worked through the PCL, including the ways the process has transformed the congregation's life. This story draws material from a variety of churches that have engaged in this process to shape the tale of the fictional Dawson United Methodist Church.

Discovery is only the beginning. Gifts must be developed and deployed in community if the congregation is to move beyond information to transformation. Chapter 6 explores this crucial aspect of the PCL process and offers ideas, questions, and discussion topics designed to allow you to customize the journey most appropriately for your congregation. While the process is initially aimed at the leadership core of the local church, it is a fine process for every Christian believer striving to find his or her place in the body of Christ and in the ministry of Christ to the world.

A series of appendixes offers a process schedule and checklist for the group leader, statistical data from the fifteen-year history of the process, a narrative, interpretive matrices of the combined results of the tools, and follow-up exercises to help integrate the discovery method into the whole church.

It is critically important to realize that strict adherence to the tools and processes listed here is not the point.[9] The tools are a means to an end. They do not yield statistically reliable or valid data. All the tools are subjective, self-reporting exercises that are intended to open people's thinking to the important issues of spiritual gifts, working styles, and ways of encountering God. Many people have used the tools as a springboard to different approaches to each topic.

Equipped for Every Good Work is the best way we know to systematically explore what it means to be Christians in community, growing as disciples, committed to a larger purpose. It is not a destination, and in fact, many churches report that they end up with more questions at the end of the process than when they began. However, they also say that the process equips them to address the questions better than ever before.

The vast majority of churches that have engaged in the PCL process tell us that the experience was extremely valuable, a few have said—initially, at least—they felt it was a waste of time, and a few more report that they are a new church because of it. One thing they all report during follow-up evaluation, however, is that once they engaged in the process, they were never the same again.

God calls us to faithful and fulfilling service in our world. We see the needs. We desire to serve. We are given all the equipment we need. *Equipped for Every Good Work* provides one way to learn to use what we've been given in the best way possible.

PROCESS OVERVIEW

Equipped for Every Good Work employs four tools that help individuals discover and understand their gifts, attitudes, beliefs, and behaviors that influence their ability to live as Christian disciples and to lead within a community of faith.

The Spiritual Gifts Inventory helps individuals to identify their God-given gifts for living faithfully as Christian disciples day by day and to find meaningful ways to use their gifts in connection with others through the community of faith. The process helps people understand the nature of spiritual gifts and ways to enhance the effectiveness of their gifts by linking together with others.

Leadership/Interaction Styles examines how people behave together in various settings. Looking at behavior, rather than personality, helps to explain what happens when we work together, why there is often tension, and how to be more effective in settings where differing styles are present. The LIS explores stylistic differences in ask/tell and people/task behaviors.

The Spirituality Web offers a way to appreciate the richness and beauty in six different approaches to and experiences of the divine, viewed through the lens of the means of grace. Deeper understanding of what it means to be a spiritual community can be achieved by identifying different ways that people relate to God.

Task Type Preferences describes four different ways that people choose to work together to perform a wide variety of jobs—short-term/long-term, large/small, hands-on/cognitive/creative, task/people. People are not all interested in working the same way.

Taken together, the four PCL tools allow individuals to better understand themselves as disciples of Jesus Christ and enable spiritual communities of faith to develop effective ministries based on identity rather than on structure. Identification and understanding of spiritual gifts, the ability to work flexibly and openly with people who do things differently, and comprehension of the varied ways that people relate to God are critical areas of learning for congregational leaders. However, the tools themselves are of less importance than the conversation they inspire.

Vitally important is the pastor's full participation in the process. This process is not a program that the pastoral leadership provides for the congregation. Following the body imagery of Paul, Christ is the head of the church and the pastor is one gifted individual—one part of the body—just like every other person. It is highly recommended that each church using *Equipped for Every Good Work* partner with another congregation so that the pastor and laity leaders from one congregation can facilitate the process for another, and then leaders from the second church can direct the process for the first church. In this way, the pastors and laypeople of each church can take the journey of exploration and discovery together, thus dispelling the myth of a clergy-laity separation. In churches where partnering is not an option, it is recommended that laity, or clergy-laity teams, provide leadership of the process. This arrangement also helps build connection and deepens understanding of the tools. Teaching others is often an effective way to learn!

Equipped for Every Good Work is a process, not a program. All exercises are designed to begin dialogue, not to label people. Ongoing use of the exercises can provide insight and understanding into areas of:

- disagreement and conflict;
- questions concerning the spiritual life;
- the needs of newcomers entering the faith community;
- identifying unique qualifications for ministry;
- our strengths and limitations for addressing need.

As we strive to break free from the malaise that permeates our church, creating structures built on gifted people and our relationships to one another offers a powerful alternative.

NOTES

1. See *Personal Styles and Effective Performance: Make Your Style Work for You,* by David W. Merrill and Roger H. Reid (Chilton Book Company, 1981).
2. See *A History of Christian Spirituality: An Analytical Introduction,* by Urban T. Holmes (Seabury, 1980).
3. See *Discover Your Spiritual Type: A Guide to Individual and Congregational Growth,* by Corinne Ware (Alban Institute, 1995).
4. *Discovering Your Spiritual Gifts: A Personal Inventory Method,* by Kenneth Cain Kinghorn (Francis Asbury Press, 1981).
5. *Gifts Discovery Workshop: Giftbook* and *Leader's Guide,* by Herb Mather (Discipleship Resources, 1985).
6. *SpiritGifts: Leader's Resources,* by Patricia D. Brown (Abingdon, 1996).
7. See *A History of Christian Spirituality: An Analytical Introduction,* by Urban T. Holmes (Seabury, 1980). Holmes also expanded his ideas on the methods of encountering God in seminar lectures in Muncie, Indiana, in 1983.
8. For those who are unable to access the Internet, support materials and handouts can be obtained by writing to Equipped for Every Good Work, P.O. Box 340003, Nashville, TN, 37203-0003 or by calling Dan Dick at (877) 899-2780, extension 7079.
9. An alternative tool for spiritual gifts discovery, the Spiritual Gifts Interview Method, is included in this resource to use in groups or settings where the longer Inventory may not work as well. Suggestions for ways to use the other tools in shorter, informal settings are also included.

CHAPTER 1

Foundations

SCRIPTURAL FOUNDATIONS

It is difficult to pinpoint when spiritual gifts ceased to define the identity and purpose of a congregation. Throughout the Ante-Nicene church (pre–A.D. 325) the early church fathers referred to the gifts of the spirit to describe the work of the various congregations. In the Pauline writings, differing lists of gifts reflected the unique personalities of the various churches. The three Pauline lists (1 Corinthians 12, Romans 12, and Ephesians 4) reveal twenty specific gifts. Here are contemporary translations by Dan Dick of the three passages and the gifts they highlight.

Romans 12:6-8

Each of us is gifted in unique ways, to the measure of grace given us by God; the gift of prophecy (speaking God's word) in proportion to one's faithfulness; the gift of servanthood, in service; the teacher, in teaching; the one who encourages, in encouragement; the giver, in generous stewardship; the leader, in diligence; the compassionate, in sacrificial kindness.

Gifts listed:
1. Prophecy
2. Servanthood
3. Teaching
4. Exhortation (Encouragement)
5. Giving
6. Leadership
7. Compassion

1 Corinthians 12:4-11

There are many different gifts, but they all emerge from one Spirit; and there are many different ways to serve, but one Lord that we all serve; there are many things we can do, but it is God who directs us to do them. Everyone has been given a spiritual gift to use for the common good. To one person the Spirit gives wisdom, and to someone else knowledge by the exact same Spirit. Another receives the gift of faith, while the same

Spirit grants gifts of healing to another. To others the Spirit grants the gift of miracle working, or prophecy, or the discernment of spirits, or speaking in other tongues, or interpreting other tongues. All of these gifts are activated by the same Spirit, who grants gifts to each person as the Spirit chooses.

Additional gifts listed:

8. Wisdom	12. Miracles
9. Knowledge	13. Discernment
10. Faith	14. Tongues
11. Healing	15. Interpretation of Tongues

1 Corinthians 12:27-31

Now you are the body of Christ, and each one of you is a member in it. God has appointed in the church first apostles, second prophets, then teachers, miracle workers, healers, helpers, administrators, and those who communicate in foreign tongues. Is everyone an apostle? Are all people prophets? teachers? miracle workers? Does everyone heal or speak in foreign tongues or interpret those tongues? While it is right and good to pursue such gifts, I will show you an even more excellent goal.

Additional gifts listed:
16. Apostleship
17. Helping/Assistance
18. Administration

Ephesians 4:11-12

The gifts that the Lord gave are these: apostleship, prophecy, evangelism, shepherding, and teaching so that everyone might equip the saints for ministry, to build up the body of Christ.

Additional gifts listed:
19. Evangelism
20. Shepherding

CULTURAL FOUNDATIONS: THREE PREMISES

Each of the gifts passages is set in a metaphor of the body of Christ as the appropriate defining image of the church. In this chapter, we will examine three premises regarding this image. First, we will explore the image as it was lived out in the Jesus and Pauline models of the church. Second, we will explore the idea that the church today is more focused on institutional maintenance than on Body-building. Third, we will look at how The United Methodist Church proposes that we in the local church live out our call to be the body of Christ in the world through our mission to make disciples of Jesus Christ.

Jesus/Pauline Models of the Church

There are two predominant models of the church reflected in the New Testament. These two models are presented as a reflection on what the authors of the New Testament reported, not as an analysis of what either Jesus Christ or the Apostle Paul intended.

The gospel authors present a Jesus model of the church that was small, flexible, and highly mobile. Where two or more gathered, there was the church. The church moved to where the people were, and it met whenever there was need. It was characterized by prayer, was Spirit-led, and existed to proclaim the good news, to teach, and to heal.

New Testament Church Models

The Pauline Model	The Jesus Model
– Stationary	– Mobile
– Congregational	– Small group
– Mechanistic	– Organic
– Shepherd/Flock	– Teacher/Disciple
– Ecclesial	– Apostolic
– Corporate structure	– Team structure
– Gifts-based	– Spirit-led

October 2000 Equipped for Every Good Work. Dan R. Dick & Barbara Miller

By contrast, the model of the church reflected in the writings of the Pauline school was institutional. Churches were planted by apostles. Very early in their history, congregations established set locations, times for meeting, and rituals. A leadership hierarchy was appointed with specific functions to perform. The primary focus and work of the congregation was determined by the gifts God granted to the members.

Most people agree that the contemporary church most closely resembles the Pauline model. It is important to realize that these models are not offered as alternatives to one another, rather they are most appropriately seen as two sides of one model. The Pauline model was a natural evolutionary extension of the Jesus model. Paul never felt that he was moving away from the essence of the church Jesus established. Both models are essential to an effective church. A vision for today's church most appropriately embraces and integrates both models.

We are not God; we are human. We are subject to fear and selfishness. We cannot be the body of Christ without Christ as the head. We are individuals, equipped by God to do that which best suits our deepest desires and the greatest needs of those around us. But we are also individuals called into community. We are commanded, urged, entreated, encouraged, persuaded to allow our spiritual gifts to be used, not for our own ends but for God's purpose—building up the body of Christ. The question we must continually ask ourselves is this: "Are we the body of Christ, gifted by God, unique and wonderful, yet not fully alive until we are linked in community—motivated by love and compelled by the power of grace to be the church in and for the world? Or are we a collection of body parts, self-absorbed and independent, loosely connected in a structure developed by our parents or grandparents, and largely unexamined for the last thirty to fifty years?"

Gifts-/Structure-Based Ministry

One significant reason churches tend to compartmentalize their ministries is that we are driven by our structures. We institutionalize our structures and programs and process people through them. For the most part, American Protestant churches are structured today as they have been for the last fifty years. The needs of structure (committees, charge conference forms, annual pledge drives for whole church budgets, and so forth) drive the ministry of the church.

This structure assumes a number of things:

The Structure-Based Church

October 2000 Equipped for Every Good Work. Dan R. Dick & Barbara Miller

- The system in place is the right one.
- The gifts and abilities of the people are not specialized, and therefore are interchangeable.
- The needs that the church serves are static and unchanging and do not need to be reexamined.
- Call and giftedness exist to serve the needs of the institution.
- The appropriate design for ministry varies little from congregation to congregation.
- Vision for ministry is limited by the constraints of the existing structures and processes (because of the first assumption—the system we have is the right one).

New ideas take time to work through the system. New members must adapt to the existing structure to fit in. Wonderful work is done in the name of Christ to help the community and church members, but there is increasingly a sense that things are not right. People are burning out. Clergy are pulled in many directions at once. New members don't seem to have the same commitment they used to. A change in pastors or a key leader marks a major change in direction. In many cases (and overall) pledges are down and membership is declining. What's wrong? The same approach we have used for years is no longer leading to growth. Why not? What has changed?

For many years, the institution of the church represented the spiritual voice of the nation. Church was recognized as the place to go in order to find God and contribute to the building of our communities. The world has changed. Institutions of all kinds are suspect, from government to schools to churches. The "Me" generation of the 1970s and 80s marked the pinnacle of American individualism and the loss of power of the institution to dictate or set standards of conduct. People now seek connection on their own terms. An institution or organization must be relevant to their lives to hold their interest and gain their support. A church that assumes people will know the rules, understand the language, and give automatic loyalty and support is probably doomed to die within the next twenty years.

People are seeking with great fervor and hunger. They are finding response in New-Age spiritualities and Eastern approaches that focus more on the individual journey of faith than on the needs of the institution. A church that provides avenues for individuals to explore their faith in the context of caring community, that encourages people to give voice to their questions and their desires and constantly challenge assumptions about what we do based on who we are, will thrive and grow.

The power of the gospel story to touch people's hearts and of the Holy Spirit to transform lives has never diminished. What has changed is the way people seek to approach and experience their relationships with God and with each other.

Spiritual gifts discovery offers us an opportunity to create a different way to organize and be in ministry. Gifts-based ministry is Bible based, but it is rare in The United Methodist Church. Most congregational leaders feel very little flexibility in designing appropriate systems for ministry beyond those prescribed by the *Book of Discipline*. Since the 1996 General Conference, local churches have more freedom than ever to redesign their ministry systems.

The Gifts-Based Church

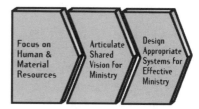

October 2000 Equipped for Every Good Work. Dan R. Dick & Barbara Miller

Gifts-based ministry focuses on the people—their gifts and passions and their sense of call and Christian vocation. It strives to develop gifts into highly effective servant skills and designs an appropriate system to deploy gifted Christians in ministry within the congregation and beyond to the community and the world.

Gifts-based ministry honors the vision and desires of individuals and creates a community where shared visions and ideas guide the work of the fellowship. There is a strong sense of the mission of the church, and the visions for ministry fall within this focal framework. The work of spiritual gifts discovery is a group activity. Tools can help the process, but nothing works better than creating environments for sharing, study, and group exploration.

Over time, the dominant gifts of a few in leadership can come to define the strengths of the congregation. It is essential to identify dominant gifts, but also to be clear about the gifts of those on the fringes of leadership. Inclusiveness depends on the commitment to expand the circle of leadership gifts.

Church leaders must assume a new role—to create and provide a safe place for the journey of faith. Leading this process of reclamation and integration requires understanding, listening skills, patience, and commitment to a shared vision. Jesus led by example,

19

inviting the disciples to "try on" ministry and return for feedback and guidance. Paul identified those gifted to lead and trusted them to do what God empowered them to do.

If our congregations are to follow God's call to discipleship, our leaders must be prepared to guide, teach, support, encourage, empower, and ultimately free them. Gifts-based ministry offers a model for living out this approach. When people who are gifted, graced, and equipped for every good work choose to live and work and grow together in community, the church is fulfilling its mission and call to love God and love neighbor through faithful discipleship.

Primary Task

The General Conference of The United Methodist Church defined the mission of the church as "to make disciples of Jesus Christ" at the 1996 session (see ¶ 120 in *The Book of Discipline, 2000*). It is important for every church to spend time discussing what the implications of this mission are and to determine how each unique congregation can best fulfill the mission.

Our *Book of Discipline* lays out a process (the primary task) for fulfilling the mission: to reach out and receive people in the name of Jesus Christ, to relate people to God, to strengthen and nurture people in the Christian faith, and to send people forth to live transformed and transforming lives in the world (see *The Book of Discipline, 2000*, ¶ 122).

A common mistake that churches sometimes make is to compartmentalize the four aspects of the primary task into separate ministry areas. They label "reaching out and receiving" as evangelism, "relating people to God" as worship, "nurturing and strengthening people in their faith" as education and formation groups, and "sending people into the world" as missions. Unfortunately, this neat separation of tasks undermines the overall mission of the church and creates division and competition between ministry groups.

Our Primary Task

Reach Out & Receive   Relate People to God

Making
Disciples

Send Forth to Live
Transformed/   Nurture & Strengthen
Transforming Lives   in the Christian Faith

October 2000 Equipped for Every Good Work. Dan R. Dick & Barbara Miller

A helpful exercise is to look at all the existing programs of the church in light of each of the four phases of the core process. Rather than asking which ministries fulfill each of the four different phases, ask how each of the ministries embodies all four of the different phases. (For instance, "How does our education program reach out and receive, relate to God, nurture and strengthen, and send forth?") Answering such questions can illuminate areas of strength and areas needing improvement.

The primary task helps us define both what we do and why we do it. Everything that we do in the church should align closely to the primary task. We most faithfully fulfill our mission when we can clearly explain how what we do reaches out and receives people, relates them to God, nurtures and strengthens them in their faith, and sends them into daily life with a clear sense of how they can be Christian disciples—of how we, together, can be the body of Christ in and for the world. The PCL is an effective lens through which to view and better understand how we are living out our collective ministry.

SPIRITUAL FOUNDATION: THE NATURE OF SPIRITUAL GIFTS

What are these gifts of the Spirit? More than just those natural abilities and talents with which we are born, more than the skills, roles, and functions that define our ministry and daily lives, the gifts of the Spirit provide the foundation for who we are as the body of Christ in Christian community and in the world. They are not given for us to boast about or to make us superior to anyone inside or beyond the faith community. They are given to us in the place and time in which we find ourselves, equipping us and empowering us, in unique ways, to do the work to which God is calling us now. These are supernatural powers—given to each and to all for the building up of the body and the kingdom.

The power of the Holy Spirit is often characterized as *ruach* (Hebrew) or *pneuma* (Greek)—the inbreathing of God. It is also represented as a burning fire. God breathed life into the first earth creature. And, at Pentecost, the rush of a mighty wind filled the house and settled as tongues of fire on the first believers, and they were filled with the Spirit (*pneuma*), transforming their lives and the world.

This power—this breath, this spark of Holy fire —is revealed in us as gifts of the spirit, or *charismata,* gifts of grace. They are within each of us, waiting and ready to guide, help, hear, and care. We have, in our busyness, largely forgotten how to listen, how to find the spark.

In Plato's myth of the cave, people are bound together in such a way that they cannot see each other. All they can see are shadows cast onto the wall of the cave in front of them. One escapes from the cave and sees the source of the shadows for the first time. That person returns to say that the real world of light and truth awaits if they are willing to struggle free of their bonds and simply turn around. Faced with the choice between appearance and the real world of full and perfect being, cave people—we—often reject the power of truth for the comfort of habit.[1] And, much like the characters in *The Wizard of Oz,* we have just the gifts we need to fulfill our deepest desires, but we are not aware of them or lack confidence in their power.

We worship and work together in the church. But how well do we really know one another? What do we know of our own or each other's deep passions, in relation to God and the world? Spiritual gifts discovery is a tool to help us begin to hear the still, small voice, to breathe in the *ruach*, the breath of God, to find and trust the spark of the Holy Spirit that will fill and empower us to: know ourselves and each other better, discern and trust God's will, and find again the joy of living in God's will for our lives.

Discovery of our individual gifts is the first step in this process. But one hot coal will not keep a fire going. Our gifts must be linked in community. When we explore our identity, our individual sense of vision for ministry is revealed. When we link our identity and call with others, we truly become church in mission and ministry. Vision that emerges from personal and community exploration fills us with shared purpose and motivates us to grow. When that exploration is filled and informed by the power of the Holy Spirit, the work of disciple making and kingdom building is energized and vital, bold and courageous. People who are excited about what they do invest deeply with time, energy, and resources.

Singers, musicians, composers, and preachers in the church develop and use their natural abilities and talents in praising God and leading others to praise God. But they don't all sing in the same style or compose the same music or preach the same sermons. There is variety in their expression.

There is also variety in the ways we are equipped and empowered by the Spirit to share the good news and make disciples. Let's look at evangelism as an example. Evangelism is an activity, a ministry of the church. Some evangelize on street corners, preaching from soapboxes. Some go door-to-door, engaging strangers in conversations about faith. Others speak to small groups, write tracts or devotional material designed for mass audiences, or live lives of Christian witness that invite others to emulate them. These are all forms of evangelism. Evangelism is also a gift of the Spirit. It is not necessary to sit on the evangelism committee to live out of Evangelism as a spiritual gift. If your talent is singing, living out of the spiritual gift of Evangelism may mean that when you sing, the power of the Spirit shines from you in a way that tells the story of grace in your life and invites others to share in it. Perhaps you choose music that tells the salvation story in powerful ways.

If you are talented as a composer with the spiritual gift of Teaching, it may be that you write music that transforms as it informs. Is your talent preaching and your spiritual gift Healing? Maybe when you preach, you soothe troubled hearts, bringing solace and peace. Whatever our talents, abilities, roles, or functions, the Spirit is working through us. We need to awaken to it, breathe it in, find the spark, share it with others. All too often, we are working rather than worshiping when we sing, read, or serve in church. How glorious it would be if we could be truly filled with holy fire in our mission and ministry, if we could trust in that power and allow God to use our spiritual gifts, working through our talents and abilities, to build up the body of Christ and prepare it to be the church in the world.

BUILDING ON THE FOUNDATION

Equipped for Every Good Work offers a process of discovering and exploring our identity as the body of Christ at a deep level. Who are we as individuals? What kind of picture emerges when we fit our pieces together? What is it that God has empowered us to be and do in this place and time? The answers—the beautiful, living tapestry revealed as we grow in knowledge and understanding—will be different for each congregation, and they will evolve and change as the congregation and the community evolve and change. Frederick Buechner reminds us that God's will resides at the meeting place of our deep passion and the deep hunger of the world.[2] The church is most effective when it attends to the needs, identity, and call of individuals, then helps link them together in community and service with one another.

Each community of faith is uniquely gifted and graced to do the work of kingdom building in its place and in its time, but we are, collectively, the body of Christ. The common thread running through all references to spiritual gifts in the biblical accounts—the essential ingredient that identified a community as Christian—is love for one another. We are the modern-day legacy of those communities. We are the heat and light of this generation. As you move through this process, open your heart to breathe in the *ruach* of life, to be transformed by the power of the Holy Spirit at work within us all.

We can reclaim our biblical roots in new ways, integrating the best of the Pauline and Jesus models and inviting individuals to deeper connection through focused exploration of their faith journey. We can learn again how to talk with one another at a deeper level and base our ministry system on what we hear. We can find new ways to listen for the call of the Holy Spirit on our lives and live more authentically out of that call as we attend to the primary task in service of our mission to make disciples of Jesus Christ.

When we are willing to love as Jesus loves, we see that real love requires an investment of our time, energy, passion, and vulnerability in building trust, respect, and joy in relationships. We can truly love one another when we make the effort and take the risk to truly know one another—as unique, beloved children of God, equipped for every good work as the body of Christ in and for the world.

NOTES

1. *The Republic,* by Plato, Book VII, vv514a-517a.
2. *Wishful Thinking: A Seeker's ABC,* revised edition, by Frederick Buechner (HarperSanFrancisco, 1993), page 119.

CHAPTER 2

Spiritual Gifts Inventory

INSTRUCTIONS FOR THE GROUP LEADER
Download Handouts and Group Process Materials from
www.equippedforeverygoodwork.org

The Spiritual Gifts Inventory is a tool for personal discovery within the context of community. It is essential to assure participants that there are no right or wrong responses. Each person will respond from a subjective context of experience, understanding, and personality.

First: Before beginning the inventory itself, distribute the handout "My Desires and God's Will." Ask the participants to take about five minutes to reflect on these questions and record their thoughts and responses:

- What do you really want? What are the deepest desires of your heart?
- What do you think or feel God wants of you?
- How are they the same or different?
- In what ways are you fulfilling your desires and God's will?
- In what ways are you blocked from doing so?

This is a purely personal exercise, intended to invite people to open to a deeper level of thought and response for the tools that follow.

Second: Distribute the "Spiritual Gifts Inventory Score Sheet" and have participants

MATERIALS
pencils
writing surface
(table groupings are best)

GROUP PROCESS MATERIALS
PCL Summary Sheet:
Putting the Pieces Together

PCL: Group Profile Grid

HANDOUTS
My Desires and
God's Will

Personal Profile Puzzle

Spiritual Gifts Inventory
Score Sheet

Spiritual Gifts
Inventory Key
and Definitions

Scripture Translations

Spiritual Gifts Clusters

Spiritual Gifts Interview
Method Score Sheet (optional)

record their names. Inform them you will be reading two hundred numbered statements. As each statement is read, the participants should record their responses in the corre-

Spiritual Gifts Inventory Score Sheet

7-Always 6-Almost Always 5-Often 4-Sometimes 3-Rarely 2-Almost Never 1-Never

1	21	41	61	81	101	121	141	161	181	1
2	22	42	62	82	102	122	142	162	182	2
3	23	43	63	83	103	123	143	163	183	3
4	24	44	64	84	104	124	144	164	184	4
5	25	45	65	85	105	125	145	165	185	5
6	26	46	66	86	106	126	146	166	186	6
7	27	47	67	87	107	127	147	167	187	7
8	28	48	68	88	108	128	148	168	188	8
9	29	49	69	89	109	129	149	169	189	9
10	30	50	70	90	110	130	150	170	190	10
11	31	51	71	91	111	131	151	171	191	11
12	32	52	72	92	112	132	152	172	192	12
13	33	53	73	93	113	133	153	173	193	13
14	34	54	74	94	114	134	154	174	194	14
15	35	55	75	95	115	135	155	175	195	15
16	36	56	76	96	116	136	156	176	196	16
17	37	57	77	97	117	137	157	177	197	17
18	38	58	78	98	118	138	158	178	198	18
19	39	59	79	99	119	139	159	179	199	19
20	40	60	80	100	120	140	160	180	200	20

NAME: _____

sponding numbered box on the score sheet according to the sliding scale (1–7) found at the top of the sheet. Boxes are numbered in vertical columns of twenty, so participants will need to record their responses by moving down, not across.

The inventory statements are read aloud in a group setting to encourage intuitive, "gut feeling" reactions, rather than thought-out responses. It is best to read each statement through twice and move on. Ask people to please hold questions and requests for clarification or repeating statements until the end of the inventory.

Another reason for administering the Spiritual Gifts Inventory in a group setting is to provide a shared experience. There will be audible responses to some of the statements, sometimes laughter. Taking the Spiritual Gifts Inventory together facilitates sharing feelings about it later. This is all part of the discovery process.

As you read the numbered statements (see pages 31-36), try not to influence response by your own preferences. Do try to vary the nuance of inflection from the first reading to the second to allow for the fullest possible understanding of meaning without further verbal explanation. Read at a fairly rapid rate and try to keep the pace moving. It takes a full hour to complete the two hundred statements (with a five- to ten-minute break after statement one hundred to flex weary hands). When you have completed all two hundred statements, people may ask for the ones they skipped along the way to be repeated. Encourage them to record a response to every statement.

There may be questions about the inventory itself. It has been reviewed by three survey designers and field tested for over fifteen years in a wide variety of settings. It is not designed or intended to be statistically or scientifically accurate. The statements have been developed from biblical and theological sources of the early Christian church. It may be observed that some of the statements do not seem to have a clean fit or that they are difficult to relate to the sliding scale. This is intentional. It reduces the potential for "psyching" or overthinking the inventory, and promotes strong either-or responses to some of the statements.

There is also some crossover between gifts in the language of the statements. The gifts are all related to one another by their purpose—building up the body of Christ for the work of ministry. As each cell within the human body has its unique function and yet shares qualities with all other cells, so too with spiritual gifts. Each has its unique place in the body of Christ, influenced by the passions and personality of the gifted individual. But all gifts are given for the common good, to lead the community of faith to maturity in love, so that we might better minister to each other and the hurting world.

Third: After the statements have all been read, have the participants add each row of ten responses across the score sheet and record the total in the boldface box at the end of the row. This is a good time to remind the group that there are no good or bad scores. High totals do not indicate increased giftedness; they may simply point to a more dramatic personal style. Some people will have totals ranging from 10 to 70. Others may not range much beyond 30 to 50.

Now is also a good time to foster community building. Some of us are good at math; some aren't. For those who complete their arithmetic task in record time, it can be a real grace to their patience, to the group, and to those who struggle for them to offer their services to someone whose math skills are not as quick. Be careful to word the suggestion in a way that does not value speed over thoroughness, but instead invites the group to be in community in terms of their various skills and abilities.

Fourth: When all the totals have been recorded, ask each person to circle the highest total. If there is a tie, they should circle all matches. Then, each person should place a check mark next to the second, third, and/or fourth highest totals. There may be ties here as well. If so, all matching totals should be included. Usually, there will be one circle and three or four check marks.

Fifth: Distribute the "Spiritual Gifts Inventory Key and Definitions" and the "Personal Profile Puzzle." Invite participants to note their primary gifts (those circled) and secondary gifts (those with a check mark) on both sheets. Note that in the early church, only primary gifts were seen as significant. Secondary gifts were ignored. Secondary gifts may

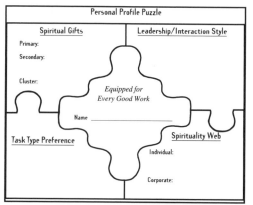

Spiritual Gifts Inventory Key an	
1. Wisdom	11. Compassion
2. Knowledge	12. Healing
3. Administration	13. Discernment
4. Apostleship	14. Teaching
5. Shepherding	15. Helping/Assist
6. Faith	16. Evangelism
7. Miracles	17. Servanthood
8. Prophecy	18. Exhortation
9. Leadership	19. Tongues
10. Giving	20. Interpretation

Administration—the gift of organizing human and materia Christ, including the ability to plan and work with peopl track progress, and evaluate the effectiveness of procedure details, communicate effectively, and take as much pleasu s they do in standing in the spotlight.

Apostleship—the gift of spreading the gospel of Jesus Ch foreign lands. Apostleship is the missionary zeal that mov uncharted territory to share the good news. Apostles emb foreign languages, visit other cultures, and go to places v opportunity to hear the Christian message. The United Sta mission field of many languages and cultures. It is no cean to enter the mission field. Even across generations, speak other languages" just to communicate.

represent those ascending or those in decline, or they may be supportive gifts for the primary gift. Focus on the primary gift and where it meets passion for service.

Make sure people have written their names on the "SGI Score Sheet" and the "Personal Profile Puzzle."

Sixth: Collect the "Personal Profile Puzzles" so you can record all of the gift data.

During a break, calculate and record the individual's gifts cluster on her or his "Personal Profile Puzzle." To determine the appropriate cluster for an individual, total the number of primary and secondary gifts listed on the puzzle, weighting primary gifts as 10 and secondary gifts as 1. (See the sidebar on the next page to learn which gifts each cluster includes.) For example, if an individual lists Healing as a primary gift and Faith, Teaching, and Exhortation as secondary gifts, the totals would be: Nurturing (2), Outreaching (10), Witnessing (13), Organizing (1). This person's gift cluster would be Witnessing. Where totals do not yield clear results, ask the individual for his or her "gut" response. Ties can remain.

On the "Group Profile Grid," list the names of all participants, recording primary and secondary gifts as well as gifts clusters for each person.

On the "PCL Summary Sheet," record totals for the group. Note patterns, clusters, and anomalies for later exploration. To determine the appropriate cluster for the group, total the top three primary gifts among all participants at 10 each and the top four secondary gifts at 1 each. This calculation should yield a clear result for the corporate cluster. Record these corporate results in the appropriate section of the "PCL Summary Sheet."

Seventh: After a break, return the Personal Profile Puzzles to the participants. Read the Scripture passages that list the twenty spiritual gifts. You may use the "Scripture Translations" (see pages 15-16 and the website). We recommend, however, setting the lists in context by sharing the entire relevant chapters (1 Corinthians 12, Romans 12, Ephesians 4) from a good translation.

Profile of Congregational Leadership: Group Profile					
Last Name	**First Name**	**Primary Spiritual Gift**	**Secondary Spiritual Gifts**	**Spiritual Gifts Cluster**	Lea Int
Anderson	Alan	Giving	Helping, Administration, Knowledge	Organizing	
Blass	Beth	Leadership	Healing, Teaching, Faith	Organizing	
Crane	Carol	Faith	Healing, Prophecy, Compassion	Witnessing	

Profile of Congregational Leadership Summary Sheet		
Putting the Pieces Together		
Spiritual Gifts	Primary	Secondary
Administration	3	12
Apostleship	0	1
Compassion	2	7
Discernment	0	6
Evangelism	0	5
Exhortation	0	4
Faith	13	22
Giving	3	7
Healing	11	19
Helping	4	10
Interpretation of Tongues	0	2
Knowledge	2	12
Leadership	1	7
Miracles	3	15
Prophecy	1	10
Servanthood	1	14
Shepherding	0	1
Teaching	6	8
Tongues	0	0
Wisdom	0	5
Spiritual Gifts Cluster		
Nurturing —152	130	22
Outreaching —158	110	48
Witnessing —341	300	41
Organizing —60	60	0
Leadership/Interaction Styles		
Director		
Dreamer		

Clusters

Congregations tend to fall into one of four distinct categories of giftedness. In alignment with language from the United Methodist *Book of Discipline*, the first three clusters are named *Nurturing, Outreaching,* and *Witnessing.* A fourth is added, *Organizing.* Wherever certain concentrations of gifts appear, the congregation displays strength in the corresponding cluster. (Provide a copy of the "Spiritual Gifts Clusters" list, available from the website, for each participant.)

The primary *Nurturing* gifts are Wisdom, Shepherding, Exhortation, Helping, Discernment, Faith, and Compassion. Nurturing congregations tend to be very committed to building fellowship, visitation, small groups, Sunday school, and member care. The mission of making disciples is primarily turned inward, and the congregational vision generally focuses on strengthening the existing fellowship.

Predominant *Outreaching* gifts include Apostleship, Evangelism, Miracles, Compassion, Healing, Servanthood, and Prophecy. Outreaching congregations tend to be missional in nature, serving the community in a variety of ways, and reaching out to people in the area. For them, disciple making is about equipping people to minister to others in the world, and their congregational vision includes images of peace, harmony, equality, and justice.

The major *Witnessing* gifts that cluster together are Knowledge, Faith, Prophecy, Teaching, Evangelism, Exhortation, and Healing. Witnessing congregations tend to emphasize worship, Christian education, and church growth, with a strong message for the masses. Faith sharing is central to the life of the fellowship, and the expectation is that they can get people to come to them. Here mission is about increasing the numbers of Christian disciples, and the vision includes an ever-expanding pool of programs and ministries that a church might provide.

Chief among the *Organizing* gifts are Knowledge, Administration, Giving, Leadership, Helping, Teaching, and Wisdom. Organizing congregations tend to be highly structured, well-organized, and program-rich. Committees and work teams involve large numbers of people. The focus is on the institution, and the mission of making disciples reflects a desire to get more people involved in leadership. The vision in most organizing churches is of financial security, strong leadership, a big building, and an active slate of programs and services.

By determining which cluster our gifts most closely align with, we can begin to understand why we do things the way we do. Most congregations that go through the PCL procedure report that the gifts clusters do more to help them understand their current reality than almost any other aspect of the process.

In the work with congregations between 1986 and 2001, Tongues and Interpretation of Tongues did not appear frequently enough to emerge in a cluster pattern. Most likely, Tongues and Interpretation of Tongues would align with Outreaching and/or Witnessing clusters.

Eighth: Now, take some time to work through the definitions for each gift. Use the "Leader's Version" of the gifts definitions as a guide (see pages 38-43). It contains some information in addition to the printed definitions given to the participants (the "Spiritual Gifts Inventory Key and Definitions" handout). You might have someone with each gift tell about his or her initial response to the definition—surprise, confirmation, or concern. In the case of ties for primary gifts, ask the person if one gift "feels" more right than the other(s). This is not exact science. It is important to link giftedness with passion for service. For summarizing what the group has learned and for reviewing the results of their work, you might also invite someone to read the paragraph profiles from the Spiritual Gifts Interview Method (pages 48-52). These thumbnail sketches will sometimes spark recognition or other responses. Talk about the group's statistical data about each gift as you go (recorded on the "PCL Summary Sheet"). How many listed each gift as primary? How many as secondary? If one of the gifts is not represented in your group, invite observation about the implications.

Ninth: Use the "Spiritual Gifts: Interpretive Helps" on pages 44-46 to help guide conversation about the spiritual gifts clusters. Discussion of the implications of these clusters can help clarify and deepen the understanding of the spiritual gifts for individuals and the group.

This is a time for open conversation. Stories, new insights, and sometimes emotions will emerge. Listen to the ways people are living out of, or are blocked from living out of, their gifts. Encourage deeper dialogue and provide a safe atmosphere for it. This opportunity for meaningful discussion is really the point of this tool and all of the PCL tools. The tools are designed to lead to deeper knowledge and appreciation of the strengths and differences that make this group uniquely equipped to do God's work.

A SPIRITUAL GIFTS INVENTORY
FOR INDIVIDUALS AND CONGREGATIONS

For each statement, rate yourself on a scale of 1 to 7.

        7 Always
        6 Almost Always
        5 Often
        4 Sometimes
        3 Rarely
        2 Almost Never
        1 Never

Inventory Statements

1. I am able to help people make choices and clarify options.
2. I am aware of things without anyone having told me about them.
3. I easily delegate authority to others.
4. I enjoy sharing my faith with the homeless and impoverished in order to give hope.
5. I enjoy teaching the Bible to a small group.
6. I believe that God will help anyone who believes in God.
7. Through prayer, God miraculously works in my life.
8. I don't mind being made fun of for what I believe.
9. I am able to organize human and material resources to serve the needs of others.
10. I enjoy giving money to support the work of God.
11. I like to work with people who are considered outcasts in their communities.
12. Praying for sick people is critical for their healing.
13. I can tell when Christian groups are being honest and faithful.
14. I listen to others as carefully as I want others to listen to me.
15. I would rather be a secretary in a group than president or chairperson.
16. When sharing my faith, I ask others about their faith commitment.
17. I help others regardless of whether they are deserving or appreciative of the help.
18. I am willing to counsel people who have spiritual, emotional, or physical problems.
19. I can speak several foreign languages.
20. I can follow the conversation of a foreign language I have never studied.
21. I am good at seeing many different sides to an issue and at helping others see them as well.
22. Things I know by faith are supported later by experience or hard data.
23. When I make decisions, I stand behind them.
24. I like being part of new ministries that didn't exist before.
25. I am an effective mentor to other Christians.

31

26. I see God's hand at work in both good times and bad.
27. God works amazing miracles in my life.
28. Others tell me that I am a good public speaker.
29. Working with a group to minister to the physical needs of others is more enjoyable than doing the same thing on my own.
30. I have enough money to give generously to important causes.
31. I like to visit people wherever they are: at home, in the hospital, in prison, and so forth.
32. I believe that God's healing power manifests itself in many different ways, not just in physical healing.
33. I am able to point out the flaw in logic of certain beliefs or teachings.
34. I need to talk about the things I read in Scripture and share my insights with others.
35. I am good at attending to details and doing "the busy work" that others often avoid.
36. An invitation to Christian discipleship should be extended to believers and nonbelievers whenever they worship.
37. I give practical/material assistance to people who are in need.
38. I will work hard for and support a group that is truly committed to its task.
39. Foreign languages are easy to learn.
40. I understand the meaning of foreign words and phrases.
41. Others are surprised by my depth of understanding and the soundness of my advice.
42. I sense people's moods and problems just by talking with them.
43. I am effective at organizing resources to minister to others.
44. I desire the opportunity to be a missionary.
45. I feel a responsibility to point out dangerous or false teachings to others.
46. I trust that God will protect those who have lost their faith.
47. I believe that God works miracles through the faith of Christian believers.
48. I find practical applications to daily life when I read the Bible.
49. It is easy for me to ask others to help with a worthy project.
50. I feel a strong desire to give money to Christian ministries.
51. I want to help anyone I can, regardless of the reason for their need.
52. I pray for the healing of those who are sick or afflicted.
53. I know when a preacher or speaker is being true to the gospel of Jesus Christ.
54. It bothers me when people are persuaded by stories of faith that contain false teachings or wrong information.
55. I give whatever time is needed to finish a project or meet a deadline.
56. I feel comfortable telling non-Christians how important it is to believe in Jesus the Christ.
57. I prefer working in the background rather than the spotlight.

58. I am patient with people who are less mature in their spirituality.
59. I communicate easily with members of other races, cultures, or generations.
60. I understand the language and attitudes of generations other than my own.
61. When others seek my advice or counsel, I am confident that my words will be sound.
62. People are surprised by how well I understand them.
63. I offer good leadership to a group or committee.
64. It is easy for me to share the gospel with other cultures that speak other languages.
65. I work to create unity and harmony within groups.
66. Regardless of the possibility or likelihood of success, I trust God's promises to be true.
67. I feel the power of the Holy Spirit when I pray.
68. My faith gives me the courage to speak out, even to people in authority.
69. I design strategies and plans for implementing ministries through the church.
70. I know whether or not an appeal for money is legitimate.
71. My compassion for others prevents me from tending to personal needs.
72. I participate in the healing of people through prayer.
73. I sense elements of truth or error in other people's teachings.
74. I enjoy creating lessons and projects that help illustrate Biblical truths.
75. Pastors and other church leaders seek my opinion on key issues.
76. I feel comfortable sharing my faith in non-Christian settings.
77. I make sure that everything runs smoothly.
78. People are willing to listen to my suggestions and criticisms because they know that I have their best interests in mind.
79. I communicate well with members of other generations.
80. I am able to interpret foreign languages for others.
81. God gives me insight into the significant decisions of others.
82. Knowing what the Bible says and means gives me the answers to my problems.
83. I help others make the most of their gifts and talents.
84. I make sure that people know I am a Christian, especially when I travel to new places.
85. I like to help others apply Christian principles to their lives.
86. Prayer on behalf of others channels God's power to their needs.
87. God uses me as an instrument of spiritual and supernatural power.
88. I see how biblical principles apply to today's world.
89. Others refer to me as an effective leader.
90. I seek the counsel of friends or family when I contribute to charity or church.
91. I listen to those who need someone to talk to.
92. When I pray, I deliberately include people who are physically or emotionally ill.
93. I know when a Christian leader is more self-interested than God-interested.
94. I need proof before I accept a claim as valid or true.

95. I am a better assistant than I am a leader.
96. The idea of sharing the gospel with other people excites me.
97. Serving others to make their lives easier is important to me.
98. People go out of their way to please me.
99. I can explain western religious practices to people of different cultures.
100. I understand intuitively the meaning of foreign rituals and practices.
101. I know some things without understanding how I know them.
102. I see potential problems that others are unaware of.
103. I focus on the big picture rather than on individual details.
104. I am accepting of different lifestyles and other cultures.
105. I look for ways to help others grow as Christian disciples.
106. I spend long periods of time in prayer for others.
107. I pray for things that other people think are impossible.
108. I enjoy showing others how the Bible speaks to their life situations.
109. I enjoy supporting ministries that help the poor and needy.
110. I am a cheerful giver of money.
111. I am drawn to people who suffer physical or emotional pain.
112. When I pray for healing for myself or others, I accept that the healing that occurs might not be the one I expect.
113. I know when people are speaking with the power of the Holy Spirit.
114. I understand the connections between the Old and New Testaments.
115. Being thanked is not important to me; I will continue to serve and give regardless of recognition.
116. It is important to me to lead others to Jesus Christ.
117. I am more interested in meeting the physical needs of others than in meeting their spiritual needs.
118. People seek out my opinion on personal matters.
119. I can speak a foreign language that I never formally studied.
120. I can accept the thoughts, speech, and actions of different cultures, even when they conflict with my own beliefs.
121. I have a clear sense of the right choices that other people should make.
122. My intuitions are clear and correct.
123. I work well under pressure.
124. I would like to represent the church in a foreign country.
125. When Christians lose faith, it is my duty to try to help them recover it.
126. Others tell me that I have a strong faith.
127. When I pray, I invoke God's power to change present circumstances.
128. I am committed to speaking the truth even when my stance is unpopular with others.
129. In a group, I emerge as a leader.

130. My money management abilities are of value to my church.
131. I am especially drawn to people who are suffering.
132. Others have told me that I have a healing touch.
133. I am deeply troubled by spiritualities that lack a sound theological basis.
134. I am energized and excited when I teach.
135. I enjoy making work easier for other people.
136. It is easy to invite people to make a commitment to Christ.
137. I prefer doing a job to planning a job.
138. Others tell me that I am a good counselor.
139. I am able to effectively communicate, in other languages, complex ideas about God.
140. I feel a close kinship with members of other cultures and traditions.
141. When I am faced with difficult choices in life, biblical applications come to mind.
142. I know when people are upset, no matter how well they try to hide it.
143. I am a good judge of other people's gifts for ministry and service.
144. I want to learn a new language in order to qualify for mission work.
145. I enjoy working with newcomers to the Christian faith.
146. I see the image of God in everyone I meet.
147. When I pray for the health of others, there are tangible results.
148. I talk to people about salvation and heaven.
149. I like directing projects better than participating in them.
150. When I give money, I give it anonymously.
151. I reach out to people who have gotten themselves in trouble.
152. When I see people in pain, I am moved to pray for them.
153. I know when someone is not being honest.
154. I would rather read Scripture or theology than Christian biographies or inspirational stories.
155. I would rather have a task defined for me than have to define it for myself.
156. I let people know what Christ has done in my life.
157. I do what is right even when it means breaking the rules.
158. I challenge people with hard truths, even if it makes me unpopular.
159. I am called to proclaim the gospel in a foreign culture or location.
160. I can translate foreign phrases into my own language automatically.
161. God allows me to see situations from God's own perspective.
162. I am able to apply difficult biblical concepts to real-life situations.
163. I encourage people to use their gifts and talents to serve others.
164. I seek the opportunity to spread the gospel to unchurched people.
165. I assist others in their discipleship journey and spiritual growth.
166. God's promises in the Bible are still valid today.
167. I help others see God's miracles when they don't see them on their own.

168. The Bible speaks directly to the economic, social, and justice issues of our day.
169. People say that I am organized.
170. There is no limit to what I will give to help others.
171. I am very sensitive to the feelings of others.
172. I encourage people to pray for the sick and the afflicted.
173. I find inspirational messages and spiritual applications in secular books, films, or speeches.
174. I read the Bible to learn and understand God's will.
175. I prefer serving to leading.
176. I talk to nonbelievers about the Christian faith and invite them to make a commitment.
177. I enjoy doing jobs that others consider less important.
178. I encourage dispirited and discouraged people whenever possible.
179. I have spoken a language without knowing what it was.
180. I can explain the theological thinking and teaching of foreign speakers to nonforeign-speaking people.
181. People tell me they are impressed by my insights.
182. I look at issues and situations from as many different angles as possible.
183. I enjoy managing people and resources.
184. I study other cultures and traditions with a hope that I might serve more people.
185. I want to get to know the people I serve and give aid to.
186. Even when others grow discouraged, it is easy for me to trust God.
187. My first reaction to problems or difficulties is to pray.
188. I believe that God speaks through me.
189. I experience my faith more in day-to-day living than in study, prayer, and reflection.
190. I am ready to give money to a cause I believe in.
191. Where there is sickness or suffering, I engage in the laying on of hands.
192. My faith increases when I witness the miracles of God.
193. People gain a clearer understanding of the Bible when I explain it to them.
194. I enjoy preparing Bible study or church school lessons.
195. I make sure everything is prepared so that meetings, programs, or services run smoothly and everyone has everything he or she needs.
196. I am more effective at sharing the gospel one-on-one than at sharing it in front of a group or crowd.
197. I minister in ways other than preaching, teaching, or praying.
198. I tell others that practicing the spiritual disciplines will help their faith grow.
199. People who speak only another language understand what I am saying.
200. I feel God leading me to involvement with people of other races, cultures, or generations.

Spiritual Gifts Inventory

Once you have completed the entire survey, total each horizontal line of the score sheet. Enter the total number in the boldface column at the end of the row. Your top score (*scores* if there is a tie) is your primary gift. The other two scores are secondary, or complementary, gifts. You can match the numbers on the score sheet with the names of the gifts using the "Spiritual Gifts Inventory Key and Definitions" handout, which also gives descriptions of each gift. A leader's version is provided on pages 38-43.

For congregations, tally the number of individuals who discovered each of the gifts as either a primary or secondary gift. The top three primary gifts provide the core congregational giftedness. The next four gifts (whether primary or secondary) provide secondary or complementary giftedness. These seven gifts can offer an indication of the gifts for ministry within a particular congregation.

SPIRITUAL GIFTS DEFINITIONS: LEADER'S VERSION

1. Wisdom	11. Compassion
2. Knowledge	12. Healing
3. Administration	13. Discernment
4. Apostleship	14. Teaching
5. Shepherding	15. Helping/Assistance
6. Faith	16. Evangelism
7. Miracles	17. Servanthood
8. Prophecy	18. Exhortation
9. Leadership	19. Tongues
10. Giving	20. Interpretation of Tongues

Administration—the gift of organizing human and material resources for the work of Christ, including the ability to plan and work with people to delegate responsibilities, track progress, and evaluate the effectiveness of procedures. Administrators attend to details, communicate effectively, and take as much pleasure in working behind the scenes as they do in standing in the spotlight.

This gift is important for the development and support of ministry programs. Administrators are able to "put the puzzle pieces together" to make things happen. They tend to be highly organized. If they don't know how to do something, they will find someone who does. They keep promises, and they stay focused and on target. They tend to be task oriented, but they value and nurture people as well. Administrators tend not to be put off by the size or difficulty of the task. It is best to give administrators their assignments, then get out of the way and let them do well what they do best.

Apostleship—the gift of spreading the gospel of Jesus Christ to other cultures and to foreign lands. Apostleship is the missionary zeal that moves us from the familiar into uncharted territory to share the good news. Apostles embrace opportunities to learn foreign languages, visit other cultures, and go to places where people have not had the opportunity to hear the Christian message. The United States of America is fast becoming a mission field of many languages and cultures. It is no longer necessary to cross an ocean to enter the mission field. Even across generations, we may find that we need to "speak other languages" just to communicate.

This gift moves us from the security of the local congregation into the unknown frontiers of the world to share the message of the Christian gospel. Apostleship is the gift that instills missionary zeal in the men and women who will go where the gospel is foreign and formerly unheard. Apostles are accepting and tolerant of cultural beliefs and practices counter to their own as a means of meeting people where they are. Once defined as a gift that took us to foreign shores, Apostleship today may mean relating to a different culture or generation that exists in our own community.

Compassion—the gift of exceptional empathy with those in need that moves us to action. More than just concern, Compassion demands that we share the suffering of others in order to connect the gospel truth with other realities of life. Compassion moves us beyond our comfort zones to offer practical, tangible aid to all God's children, regardless of the worthiness of the recipients or the response we receive for our service.

This gift moves congregational members outside of themselves and the constraints of the church facility to put faith into action. Compassion motivates people to sacrificial service and helps to provide caregiving within and beyond the local church. Compassion as a spiritual gift generally ranks low among United Methodist churches.

Discernment—the ability to separate truth from erroneous teachings and to rely on spiritual intuition to know what God is calling us to do. Discernment allows us to focus on what is truly important and to ignore that which deflects us from faithful obedience to God. Discernment aids us in knowing whom to listen to and whom to avoid.

This gift helps congregations make good choices in selecting leaders, setting priorities, and analyzing how to accomplish tasks. Intuitive by nature, Discernment safeguards the church leadership from making unwise decisions. Discernment is also a vital gift for settling disputes.

Evangelism—the ability to share the gospel of Jesus Christ with those who have not heard it before or with those who have not yet made a decision for Christ. This gift is manifested in both one-on-one situations and in group settings, both large and small. Evangelism is an intimate relationship with another person or persons that requires the sharing of personal faith experience and a call for a response of faith to God.

Once the cornerstone of the Methodist movement, Evangelism has fallen on hard times in The United Methodist Church. We are no longer thought of as an evangelistic church, and our faith sharing tends to be "preaching to the choir" instead of taking the message out to the world. Disciple making is dependent upon Evangelism, in all its many forms.

Exhortation—the gift of exceptional encouragement. Exhorters see the silver lining in every cloud, offer deep and inspiring hope to the fellowship, and look for and commend the best in everyone. Exhorters empower others to feel good about themselves and to feel hopeful for the future. Exhorters are not concerned by appearances; they hold fast to what they know to be true and right and good.

Beyond exceptional hopefulness and the ability to hold forth support and encouragement in difficult situations, Exhortation is a gift of wise counsel, speaking the truth in love, holding one another accountable, and extending the hand of forgiveness. Traditionally, Exhortation has not been highly valued in The United Methodist Church, and thus people with this gift often do not land in leadership positions.

Faith—the exceptional ability to hold fast to the truth of God in Jesus Christ in spite of pressures, problems, and obstacles to faithfulness. More than just belief, Faith is a gift that empowers an individual or a group to hold fast to its identity in Christ in the face of any challenge. The gift of Faith enables believers to rise above pressures and problems that might otherwise cripple them. Faith is characterized by an unshakable trust in God to deliver on God's promises, no matter what. The gift of Faith inspires those who might be tempted to give up to hold on.

Those gifted with Faith create a foundation upon which true community can be built and sustained. It is critical for people possessing the gift of Faith to make opportunities to share their beliefs, their learning, and, most importantly, their life experiences. Faith stories have powerful and transforming effects. Faith is usually a prominent gift in witnessing congregations, where personal stories are often shared in group settings, worship, Sunday school classes, and Bible studies.

Giving—the gift of the ability to manage money to the honor and glory of God. Beyond the regular response of gratitude to God that all believers make, those with the gift of Giving can discern the best ways to put money to work, can understand the validity and practicality of appeals for funds, and can guide others in the most faithful methods for managing their financial concerns.

Giving is about faithfulness, desire, and ability to manage funds as much as it is about donating money to the church. People with the gift of Giving need to be placed in positions where money is given, raised, and distributed. Those thus gifted need to be allowed to take both responsibility and authority for the finances of the community of faith. Gifted givers are often inspirational models to others of what it means to be generous.

Healing—the gift of conducting God's healing powers into the lives of God's people. Physical, emotional, spiritual, and psychological healing are all ways that healers manifest this gift. Healers are prayerful, and they help people understand that healing is in the hands of God. Often their task is to bring about such understanding more than it is to simply erase negative symptoms. Some of the most powerful healers display some of the most heartbreaking afflictions themselves.

Emotional and spiritual healing are as critical in our day as physical healing. Those who can speak healing words and care for the social and emotional needs of the community of faith build strong congregations. Healing ministries tend to be growth ministries, especially when the vision extends beyond the local church. Healing takes many forms—internal healing is vitally important for church health, while external healing is a critical ministry to the world.

Helping—the gift of making sure that everything is ready for the work of Christ to occur. Helpers assist others to accomplish the work of God. These unsung heroes work behind the scenes and attend to details that others would rather not be bothered with.

Helpers function faithfully, regardless of the credit or attention they receive. Helpers provide the framework upon which the ministry of the body of Christ is built.

The key to effective leadership is empowered followers who can offer support and organization to the front line. Without gifted helpers, few churches have what it takes to maintain growing, effective ministry. Helping should be regarded as a valuable gift in and of itself. Too often we move gifted helpers to leadership positions where they do not function as successfully.

Interpretation of Tongues (*see also* Tongues)—the gift of (1) the ability to interpret foreign languages without the necessity of formal study in order to communicate with those who have not heard the Christian message or who seek to understand, or (2) the ability to interpret the gift of Tongues as a secret prayer language that communicates with God at a deep spiritual level. Both understandings of the gift of Interpretation of Tongues are communal in nature: the first extends the good news into the world; the second strengthens the faith within the fellowship.

Similar to Tongues in that it is not highly represented in The United Methodist Church, Interpretation allows people to understand members of other cultures, generations, and ethnicities.

Knowledge—the gift of knowing the truth through faithful study of Scripture and the human situation. Knowledge provides the information necessary for the transformation of the world and the formation of the body of Christ. Those possessing the gift of Knowledge challenge the fellowship to improve itself through study, reading of Scripture, discussion, and prayer.

This gift allows churches to teach and function at a high level, doing a variety of programs and ministries and working to develop multiple levels of education, worship, and service. Knowledge provides a firm foundation for education ministries and is critical for shared leadership and team-based ministry.

Leadership—the gift of orchestrating the gifts and resources of others to accomplish the work of God. Leaders move people toward a God-given vision of service, and they enable others to use their gifts to the best of their abilities. Leaders are capable of creating synergy, whereby a group achieves much more than its individual members could achieve on their own.

Leadership is a critical function within the congregation that often falls to the pastor by default. While the pastor must assume many leadership roles, the true gift of Leadership can provide vision and direction to the congregation that one pastor alone cannot manage. Many pastors have reported that their job became much easier when they got out of the way and allowed those more gifted in Leadership to take a more directive role. Pastors should look to work in partnership with their most gifted leaders. Leadership is not the management of ministry. Leaders need to be doing the visioning and strategic planning work of the community of faith. Leaders focus on the future and the best way to build bridges from the current reality to the desired reality for the congregation.

Miracles—the gift of an ability to operate at a spiritual level that recognizes the miraculous work of God in the world. Miracle workers invoke God's power to accomplish that which appears impossible or impractical by worldly standards. Miracle workers remind us of the extraordinary nature of the ordinary world, thereby increasing faithfulness and trust in God. Miracle workers pray for God to work in the lives of others, and they feel no sense of surprise when their prayers are answered.

This gift is not about performing miracles as much as it is about acknowledging the miraculous power of God in the church and in the world. By living in the miracle power of God, this gift allows people to rise above the ordinary to see the extraordinary nature of daily living. Miracles is a gift that empowers congregations to witness to the truth of Christ in the world.

Prophecy—the gift of speaking the word of God clearly and faithfully. Prophets allow God to speak through them to communicate the message that people most need to hear. While often unpopular, prophets are able to say what needs to be said because of the spiritual empowerment they receive. Prophets do not foretell the future, but they proclaim God's future by revealing God's perspective on our current reality.

Prophets do not so much speak for God as allow God to speak through them. Prophecy has nothing to do with foretelling the future; it is instead about forth-telling the truth in love. Prophets are often respected despite being unpopular. Prophets often focus on the task at hand more readily than the people served. Often prophets are dismissed easily, since much of what they say flies in the face of conventional wisdom and communal tradition.

Servanthood—the gift of serving the spiritual and material needs of other people. Servants understand their role in the body of Christ to be that of giving comfort and aid to all who are in need. Servants look to the needs of others rather than focusing on their own needs. To serve is to put faith into action; it is to treat others as if they were Jesus Christ. The gift of service extends our Christian love into the world.

This gift moves people beyond their own needs and the needs of the local congregation to move in active service into the community and world. Servants sacrifice personal comfort and care for the needs of others. Servants give the church its reputation for care, mercy, and justice in the world.

Shepherding—the gift of guidance. Shepherds nurture others in the Christian faith and provide a mentoring relationship to those who are new to the faith. Displaying an unusual spiritual maturity, shepherds share from their experience and learning to facilitate the spiritual growth and development of others. Shepherds take individuals under their care and walk with them on their spiritual journeys. Many shepherds provide spiritual direction and guidance to a wide variety of believers.

This gift is primarily a mentoring gift where the shepherd works with individuals or small groups to empower them to live as faithful disciples in the world. Shepherds take others under their wing to help them maximize their potential.

Teaching—the gift of bringing scriptural and spiritual truths to others. More than just teaching Christian education classes, teachers witness to the truth of Jesus Christ in a variety of ways, and they help others to understand the complex realities of the Christian faith. Teachers are revealers. They shine the light of understanding into the darkness of doubt and ignorance. They open people to new truths, and they challenge people to be more in the future than they have been in the past.

Because we have been a "Sunday school denomination," many of our churches uncritically provide Christian education without careful consideration of the appropriate leadership. Teaching is a gift, and without the gift education can become a chore for leaders and an endurance test for students. Recruiting nonteachers to teach has consistently undermined our Christian education efforts throughout the church. Let the teachers teach and allow nonteachers to find another way to serve. It is better to combine classes under a gifted teacher than to inflict nongifted teachers on unsuspecting classes just to fill out the roster.

Tongues (*see also* Interpretation of Tongues)—the gift of (1) the ability to communicate the gospel to other people in a foreign language without the benefit of having studied said language (see Acts 2:4) or (2) the ability to speak to God in a secret, unknown prayer language that can only be understood by a person possessing the gift of Interpretation. The ability to speak in the language of another culture makes the gift of Tongues valuable for spreading the gospel throughout the world, while the gift of speaking a secret prayer language offers the opportunity to build faithfulness within a community of faith.

Not highly represented in The United Methodist Church today, Tongues is not just about foreign languages. It is about being able to communicate across a wide variety of cultural and generational barriers.

Wisdom—the gift of translating life experience into spiritual truth and of seeing the application of scriptural truth to daily living. The wise in our faith communities offer balance and understanding that transcend reason. Wisdom applies a God-given common sense to our understanding of God's will. Wisdom helps us remain focused on the important work of God, and it enables newer, less mature Christians to benefit from those who have been blessed by God to share deep truths.

Experience is the best teacher, and the ability to apply biblical concepts and truths to the day-to-day living of members of the community of faith is critical. If we lack one thing in The United Methodist Church today, it may well be basic common sense. Those with the gift of Wisdom provide us with much needed common sense.

SPIRITUAL GIFTS: INTERPRETIVE HELPS

General Questions for Discussion and Reflection

- In what areas of ministry are we clearly utilizing and honoring our spiritual gifts?
- What are we attempting to do in ministry that we may not be strongly gifted for?
- How do we fully honor the giftedness of those who do not share the dominant gifts of our current leadership?
- What do we currently have in place in our church program to develop the spiritual gifts of our congregation? What might we need to develop?
- How can we encourage others in our congregation to explore their spiritual giftedness for ministry?
- Do these spiritual gifts lists raise any concerns for us? Do they generate any thoughts, feelings, or ideas?

Cluster Questions and Reflections

Nurturing

- In what ways do we experience fellowship for fellowship's sake? (In other words, in what ways do we experience fellowship without a program, a study, or a task connected with it?)
- Are there segments of our membership that we do not know much about? How can we find out about these groups?
- What is our relationship with the less active/inactive members?
- What methods and systems do we employ to bring people together in order to deepen relationships and build community?
- Who does visitation within our congregation? What is the nature of our visits? How do we welcome and include visitors?
- One helpful determining factor that differentiates nurturing churches from witnessing churches is the way they view visitation and member care. Nurturing congregations seldom have visitation or membership committees. It is understood that visiting and member care are included in all areas of ministry. Witnessing congregations usually form committees and have training for visitation and networks for member care. Which view describes our church?

Outreaching

- In what ways does our community depend upon our church's ministries and services?
- What is our evangelistic witness/message? How is it delivered?
- Is our long-range vision for the congregation church-centered, community-centered, or world-centered?
- What proportion of our program and budget (apart from apportioned funds) is designated for foreign missions? domestic missions? local missions?

- How are peace, justice, and political issues addressed within the congregation?
- What proportion of our energies and resources is tied into maintenance of our facility, staff, and program?
- What systems and processes are in place to help educate, train, and deploy stewards for missional work beyond the congregation?
- As these questions are discussed, it is well to ask, "Are we gifted to make a difference in these areas? Where might we best use our gifts to make the largest impact on our fellowship, our community, and our world?"

Witnessing

- Does our existing structure for ministry fully utilize the predominant gifts of our congregation?
- Have we maximized our potential by providing a variety of worship opportunities aimed at the diversity within our community? How might we extend our services in these ways?
- What opportunities do we offer for people to discuss their faith questions openly and to receive guidance and nurture?
- In what ways do our organizational structures promote faith development and growth in discipleship? In what ways might our structures obstruct or prevent faith development and growth in discipleship?
- What do we believe the central mission of the church to be? How are we fulfilling that mission at this time? What do we need to do to more effectively fulfill that mission in the future?
- How can we best utilize the gifts of our cluster to improve the ministries of the church? (Do we have the right people in the right places? Are there things we are doing that we should give up in order to free some people for more effective service?)

Organizing

- How much of our time and energy is focused on structure for effective ministry?
- In what ways are we structured for the sake of being effectively structured?
- Do our members with gifts in leadership, administration, giving, serving, and wisdom feel that their talents are being well used? (Ask them.)
- What do the movers and shakers of the congregation believe they are moving and shaking? (To what end are they using their talents?)
- How many positions of leadership is one person allowed to hold in the church?
- Effective members with organizing gifts often find themselves rewarded for their effectiveness with ever-increasing responsibility, thus limiting their overall effectiveness. (Go figure.) How do we recognize and reward effective ministry?

- Are the members most gifted in organizing ministries well represented on the committee on lay leadership? (Just a suggestion.)
- What ministries would cease, or greatly diminish in quality, if the supporting committee were to go out of existence? (That is, if there were no worship committee, what would the impact be on worship; if there were no education committee, the impact on education; and so forth.)

SPIRITUAL GIFTS INTERVIEW METHOD

While it is highly recommended that the Spiritual Gifts Inventory be used whenever possible, the Interview Method is provided here as an alternative for those who feel the Spiritual Gifts Inventory is simply too long or detailed for a particular group. The Interview Method is a collection of twenty paragraphs that provide thumbnail sketches of each gift. It has been suggested that you might use the paragraphs as part of the exploration and discovery after completing the Spiritual Gifts Inventory, but the Interview Method can also be used on its own when time is a critical factor and for groups beyond the active leadership.

Most participants find the Spiritual Gifts Inventory more satisfying because of their active involvement in the process; the shorter time requirement of the Interview Method is its main advantage. The Interview Method will effectively reveal patterns and strengths for individuals and help begin the dialogue of discovery. It is, however, much less detailed and precise than the Spiritual Gifts Inventory. Differentiation among gifts will not be as apparent.

After completing the "My Desires and God's Will" exercise, distribute the Spiritual Gifts Interview Method Scoring Sheets (from the website). Have participants listen as you read each numbered paragraph all the way through before recording their reactions. They should use the sliding scale (5-1) printed at the top of the score sheet. It is important that they respond to the overall paragraph, not isolated sentences within it.

It takes about thirty to forty minutes to complete the interview. Participants should then circle any 5's or 4's they have recorded. Use the Spiritual Gifts Inventory Key to identify the names of the gifts described in the paragraphs, and then read aloud the Spiritual Gifts Definitions. As the group reviews the definitions together, one gift may begin to "feel" more right than others. That gift should be marked with an asterisk.

Collect the scoring sheets after the discussion, and note the results on the "PCL: Group Profile Grid" and the "PCL Summary Sheet." Be sure to allow time to discuss patterns, clusters, and anomalies.

Spiritual Gifts Interview Method Score Sheet

Name:_____

Place the appropriate number in the score box for each paragraph. Circle all fives, and place a star or check mark beside all fours. The leader will provide the key and definitions for the twenty gifts. Write the name of the gifts in the spaces for all fives and fours. These will highlight your primary and secondary gifts.

5   *This paragraph describes me exactly*
4   *This paragraph describes me very well*
3   *This paragraph describes me a little*
2   *This paragraph barely describes me*
1   *This paragraph doesn't describe me at all*

Paragraph #	Score	Gift (see Key)
1		
2		
3		
4		
5		
6		
7		
8		
9		
10		
11		
12		
13		
14		
15		
16		
17		
18		
19		
20		

A Spiritual Gifts Interview Method for Individuals and Congregations

Listen to or read each of the following paragraphs. On your scoring sheet, mark the answer that you most strongly agree with. Think about how the entire statement applies to your life. Respond to the entire paragraph, not just sentences within the paragraph.

1. People are often surprised at how well I understand what they are going through. Many people seek my advice and know that they can count on me to tell the truth and not just try to tell them what they want to hear. God often helps me know just the right thing to say to people who ask me for my opinion. Sometimes I even understand a problem before anyone explains it to me. I can usually see where the Bible applies to other people's situations, and often it is clear to me what another person should do even when it isn't clear to him or her. Other people have told me that I am perceptive and insightful.

2. I am both an intuitive person and a good problem solver. When logic fails, I can still figure out solutions to difficult problems. The Bible often gives me direction to solve problems. I can look at a situation and immediately understand how it happened, and I usually have a good idea about how to deal with it. If there is a project to do, I am good at laying out exactly what will be needed to complete the task. I am always learning new ways to deal with new situations. I have a good memory and am able to steer clear of repeating mistakes. Others often seek from me answers to questions that they cannot figure out.

3. I am good at getting things done. I am organized. I delegate responsibility to others, and I have a clear sense of what needs to get done and when it needs to be done. I am skilled at running a meeting, and I rarely go into a situation without all the information I need to make decisions. I have the ability to bring the right people together to get a job done, and I am very perceptive about the skills and abilities people bring to a task. When there is paperwork to be done or reports to fill out and file, I will be sure that they are done properly. I tend to look at the big picture, making sure that everything is covered and that nothing is overlooked. I try to make sure that supplies never run out, instructions are clear and understood, and jobs get done on time.

4. I believe that faith means action. I want to serve God by serving the needs of others, especially when the people are of a different race or culture. It is exciting to talk about Jesus and the Christian faith to people who have never heard about them before. I would be willing to learn another language in order to take the gospel to people in other countries. Mission projects and missionary work excite me. I think that God really wants me to work with people who are very different from what I am used to. I think it would be exciting to start a new church in another country. I would like to travel in order to spread the gospel of Jesus Christ.

5. I believe in building strong community within the church. I especially like working in small groups, and I like talking to other people one-on-one. I enjoy mentoring new or young Christians, and I feel called to talk to people who are struggling with their faith. I want to get to know people well and to help them in their faith development. I have felt compelled to point out wrong or potentially dangerous thinking to people in my church. I enjoy studying the Bible in a small group, and even if I don't lead the group I feel that I have a lot to share with others in the group. I believe I can do the greatest good one person at a time.

6. I trust God no matter what is happening in my life. When things are difficult, I spend much time in prayer. I believe that no matter what things look like, God is still in charge. When other people's faith is shaken, my faith stays strong. I often give comfort and hope to other people. I usually can see the image of God in the faces of other people, and I tend to believe the best of others. I believe that the Bible speaks as strongly to issues of our day as it has in the past. While many things in life are uncertain, God never changes. For that reason my faith stays steady and rock solid. I never question or doubt, but in all things I hold strong to my knowledge that God loves me. Other people have told me that I have a strong faith.

7. I have seen God work miracles in my own life and the lives of other people. Even in the face of impossible situations, my first response is to pray for God to intervene. I believe in the power of the Holy Spirit to work in our world. I believe in the laying on of hands as a means for God to heal people. I don't believe there are hopeless cases as long as God is involved. I believe that many miracles are blocked by the unbelief of people today. Many times I have prayed for things that seemed irrational but which happened anyway. There have been times when I was able to say or do the right thing that helped heal someone emotionally.

8. I believe that God stills speaks new messages through men and women today. I think that God wants me to speak out against things that are wrong in the world. The Bible is relevant to life today, and people need to stand up for biblical truths. Peace and justice issues are among the most important obligations for Christians today. I have the ability to articulate my beliefs, and I am a good public speaker. I am not afraid to say it when I think something is wrong, and I don't care if other people make fun of me for my beliefs. I enjoy telling other people I am a Christian, and I have no patience with people who call themselves Christian and then live and act in un-Christian ways.

9. I am an excellent organizer. I have good people skills and am able to bring out the best in people. I encourage people to develop and use their skills, and I am glad to hand off tasks to other people who can do them as well as, if not better than, I can. I am decisive and rarely worry about making the right choice. I gain other people's

respect easily. I have a clear sense of values and a vision for my life that I share freely with others. I am as interested in the success of others as I am in my own success. I am more effective working in a group than I am on my own. One of my greatest desires is to help other people realize their full potential.

10. I believe that God blesses us with money in order that we might bless others. I feel happiest when I have given something to help another person. I am a cheerful giver. I never resent the church for asking me to give. I am usually very careful about responding to appeals for money, and I am good at judging the validity of an appeal. I talk freely about money and giving with others. I encourage others to give as they are able. I don't believe that there should be a standard or a limit to what people should give. God has given me the ability to make money and the opportunities to give my money. It makes me feel good to be a generous person, but I don't make a big deal about my giving. Most of my giving is anonymous, between me and God.

11. I am sensitive to the needs of others. I believe that God wants us to respond to human need wherever we find it. Visitation to the sick, the homebound, the elderly, and the outcast is the most important ministry of the church. It is more important to serve the needs of others than my own needs. I don't care whether a person deserves help or not—if the person is needy, then I want to help. My heart breaks when I see a homeless or hungry person. I believe that the church should be doing more to help needy people. The Bible instructs us to make serving the needs of the hungry, thirsty, naked, sick, and imprisoned our primary function. I am known for my kindness.

12. I believe people can be healed by God through prayer. Faith is an important part of healing. I will pray for people who are sick or afflicted, and I know that my prayers help the situation. Miraculous healing still happens all the time. I believe that some people have the gift of healing. People have told me that I have a healing touch. Emotional and physical illness is no match for the power of God. I have been a channel for God's healing power through prayer. It is important for a church to have a group that prays for the healing and comfort of the afflicted. It is important to understand that what the healing God sends is sometimes not the healing that we asked for.

13. I have a good sense of whether someone is being honest or not. I have a keen ability to see through deception. I am often amazed by the mindless way people will follow a new fad or fashion. I have a strong intuition of whether someone is being faithful to Scripture. I can see through self-interested people instantly. I often see the potential in other people that they cannot see themselves. Many times when people say one thing, I can tell they mean something completely different. I can always tell when praise is sincere. I am often overwhelmed by a feeling that I am, or the group

I am a part of is, headed in the wrong direction. People are often amazed that I have caught something that no one else saw or thought about.

14. I believe that to have a strong faith it is vital to study and understand the Bible. I have a need to share what I learn with others, and I enjoy talking about what the Bible means. I like preparing a lesson plan for a Sunday school class or organizing my thoughts into a carefully planned presentation. I want to know what the Bible has to do with my life today. I want to help other people understand what the Bible says to them. I do not approve of taking Bible stories out of context in order to make the Scriptures say what you want them to. I want to help people understand why bad teaching and new-age "pop" spirituality are so dangerous. I enjoy unlocking the mysteries of our faith so that others grow spiritually.

15. I am a good follower, but I want to do something meaningful. While I am not an especially good leader, I am a hard worker and I can follow instructions well. I am organized and pride myself on making things easier for other people. I am an excellent assistant, and I work well with others. I don't seek praise or attention for what I do, as long as the job gets done well. I like serving the needs of other people, and I am perfectly content to stay behind the scenes and out of the spotlight. I have a gift for making preparations and focusing on detail. Other people often seek my advice on the best way to do something, and I am often asked to be part of a planning group or committee. I enjoy being helpful.

16. Sharing my faith with other people is important to me, and I find it easy to do. When I talk about my faith, I want others to talk about theirs. I feel comfortable challenging someone to make a commitment to Christ. I like talking to Christians and non-Christians alike. I am not threatened by talking with someone of another faith, and I respect their differences. I look for opportunities to share the gospel with other people. I would give a Bible to a stranger and encourage him or her to read it. I feel that my call is to go and make disciples in the world. I feel much more comfortable talking about my faith one-on-one than in front of a group. I believe that the church is out in the world where two or more are gathered to talk about Jesus Christ.

17. I am a doer rather than a thinker/planner. I would rather serve someone's physical needs and leave other people to address their spiritual needs. I have a difficult time talking about my faith, but I am motivated by my faith to help others in need. I will gladly work on a project or a job, but I would rather not serve in planning the work. I believe that the way I live my life is a more powerful testimony to my faith than anything I could say. My faith is a private matter, but I believe that God wants me to help others and serve the needy. I don't ask many questions, but am always ready to respond to the questions of others.

18. I am a cheerleader in the church, but I am also very honest. I try to encourage people when they are down, but I also challenge them to do better. I have been told that I am a good counselor and that I can be trusted. People respect my opinion because they know that I am both honest and concerned for their well-being. People seek out my opinion, and they often open up to me with their deepest concerns. I often find myself in the position of saying things that aren't popular or politically correct because others are afraid of hurting feelings. I will tell people when I think they are wrong but am also the first to tell them they are right or to give them praise.

19. I can speak several languages fluently and find foreign languages very easy to learn. I communicate very well with members of different cultures and across generations. I like to explain Western religious practices to other ethnic groups. I can communicate easily in a language I have never formally studied. I do not find language a barrier to communicating complex theological concepts. I feel led to proclaim the gospel in a foreign land. I have spoken a language without knowing what it was. People who speak only in another language can understand what I say.

20. I can follow the conversations of people speaking a foreign language, even though I haven't studied their language. I have an intuitive understanding of foreign words and phrases. I understand the language of other nations, races, and generations, even when it is quite different from my own. I can interpret foreign languages for others. I have an intuitive grasp of foreign rituals and practices. I have no problem accepting other people's thinking, speaking, and acting when these conflict with my personal beliefs. I feel a close kinship with members of other cultures and traditions. I can translate English and foreign phrases automatically. I can explain the theological thinking and teaching of foreign speakers to nonforeign-speaking people. I feel God leading me to involvement with people of other races, cultures, and generations.

CHAPTER 3

Leadership/Interaction Styles

INSTRUCTIONS FOR THE GROUP LEADER
Download Handouts and Group Process Materials from
www.equippedforeverygoodwork.org

The second Profile of Congregational Leadership (PCL) tool, Leadership/Interaction Styles, adds dimension to our picture of the group or church. While the Spiritual Gifts Inventory names the spiritual dimension of our relationships, the Leadership/Interaction Styles tool points to the ways we behave with one another. It is in our interactions that our gifts are seen, known, and cherished—or blocked and ignored. The Leadership/Interaction Styles tool helps to reveal why we work as we do and to further our ability to truly know and appreciate one another as multidimensional and valuable.

Remember, we are exploring behavior, not personality. Sometimes, the setting in which we find ourselves will cause us to behave in ways that our personality would not necessarily indicate. Because of this, it is essential to gather input from others who know us and have observed us interacting in a group setting. Comparing how others see us with the way we see ourselves is valuable in deepening our self-knowledge.

MATERIALS

pencils

writing surface
(table groupings are best)

GROUP PROCESS MATERIALS

Personal Profile Puzzle

PCL Summary Sheet: Putting the Pieces Together

PCL: Group Profile Grid

HANDOUTS

Leadership/Interaction Styles Introduction

Characteristics of the Leadership/Interaction Styles

Stress Paths of Leadership/Interaction Styles

Harmonizing the Leadership/Interaction Styles

First: Return the Personal Profile Puzzles that were completed while working on the Spiritual Gifts Inventory. Participants will use them to record the results of the Leadership/Interaction Styles tool. Distribute the "Characteristics of the Leadership/Interaction Styles" worksheets and make sure people write their names at the top.

Briefly examine the "Leadership/Interaction Styles Introduction" (page 57; also available from the website), being sure to emphasize the intrinsic value of and need for all four styles in effective ministry and mission. Read through the "Descriptive Statements of the Leadership/Interaction Styles" (pages 58-60). Invite participants to record strong responses on sheets beside the characteristics. There will be recognition and confirmation for some; surprise for others. The following illustration offers a lighthearted perspective on the styles.

Characteristics of the Leadership/Interaction Styles

NAME:_____

Thinker	Director
• Laid-back	• Task-oriented
• Deliberate	• Decisive
• Logical	• Energetic
• Values facts, figures, data	• Focused on results
• Quiet	• Time-conscious
• Likes to examine multiple options/angles	• Risk-taking
• Enjoys argument/debate	• Has considerable self-confidence
• Cautious	• Acts quickly
• Needs time for decisions/judgments	• Highly organized
• Exacting	• Hates to waste time
• Focused on end results	• Expects concurrence
• Hides feelings	• Values reason
• Highly organized	• Gets down to business quickly
• Withholds opinions	• Agenda/calendar–bound
• Task oriented	• Wants fast answers/response
• Slow to decide	• Uses clear, concise language
• Sticks to schedules/outlines/plans	• Logical, linear thinker
• Good at planning	• Highly opinionated

Pleaser	Dreamer
• People-oriented	• Outgoing
• Diplomatic	• Creative
• Very flexible	• Loves a good time
• Loves to help	• Focused on big picture
• Holds agenda secondary to relationships	• People-oriented
• Sensitive	• Seeks lots of eye contact
• Dislikes conflict/confrontation	• Talkative
• Hard-working	• Expressive/Dramatic
• Reliable	• Competitive
• Wants everyone to be happy	• Very sociable
• Makes/keeps peace	• Persuasive
• Honest	• Uses lots of gestures while speaking
• Listens well	• Opinionated
• Acts as problem solver	• Doesn't always keep promises
• Wants to be liked	• Uses visual images
• Slow-paced	• Annoyed by logic
• Likes to chit-chat	• Doesn't know what calendar/clock is for
• Loyal	• Spontaneous
• Not constrained by clock/calendar	• Enthusiastic

Bubble Gum Interaction Styles

In 1993 Dan worked with a group of management-level executives at a candy company in the northeastern United States. At one of the breaks, as a treat, someone brought in a basket filled with bubble gum. The group decided to have a bubble-blowing contest. Four of the participants in the workshop inadvertently provided a beautiful illustration of the four Leadership/Interaction Styles in action.

Robert—a Director—entered the bubble gum competition wanting to set the rules. He organized the event, lining everyone up and setting the roster of who would blow first, second, and so forth. He found a stopwatch to time the blowing time and a caliper to measure bubble size. Throughout the break, Robert chewed forcefully, steadily, purposefully.

Kate—the Dreamer—thought there should be prizes and pictures taken. She developed a cheer for the group to chant while people blew their bubbles. Halfway through each idea, Kate would say, "No, wait. I have another idea—oh, this is better, wait—this is great!" Kate chomped her gum, popping and smacking it with gusto.

Eddie—the Pleaser—wanted to make sure that everyone got a turn, and that people who didn't want to compete didn't feel like they had to. As each person took a turn, it was Eddie's voice you would hear saying, "Ooh, good bubble. Look at that one. That's a winner." Eddie chewed with an easy, slowly modulated pace. And, oh yeah, Eddie took the pictures for Kate.

Susan—the Thinker—never moved from her seat. She watched the proceedings, usually with a smile on her face. She said not a word, except to decline from competition. After about five minutes, Susan kept looking at her watch, furrowing her brow. It was clear that with each passing moment, Susan was enjoying our foolishness less and less. Susan would chew her gum a time or two—pause—then chew again, very deliberately and thoughtfully. As soon as the break was over, Susan discreetly placed her chewed gum back in the wrapper she had carefully folded and preserved.

Second: Ask the group to self-select into groups of three to five people. Encourage them to form groups with people they believe know them well. In these small groups, each person, in turn, will state what he or she believes is his or her dominant Leadership/Interaction Style. Then the others in the group will have sixty seconds each to agree or disagree. Because we are exploring behavior, not just personality, the group will often recognize an individual's style more readily than he or she does. During this talking time, the subject will simply receive the responses. Group consensus will determine the dominant style recorded on the Personal Profile Puzzle. Continue in this way around the group until every person has named his or her own style and has received responses from the full group. In a group of five, this entire process should take about twenty-five minutes.

Third: Reconvene and allow a short time for naming insights from the small-group exercise. Then distribute the "Stress Paths of Leadership/Interaction Styles" sheet (available from the website).

Take some time to help the group understand what the stress path diagrams illustrate. Use the examples on pages 61-62 to help describe what the diagrams show. Point out the stress paths for Thinkers and for Pleasers. Let the group talk about these stress paths to be sure that they understand the concept.

Explain that we all live with mild to moderate stress, and our behaviors reflect this stress. If some participants have been surprised by the dominant style revealed in their small groups, it may be that their stress levels are consistently high in certain settings. This fact can be a moment of true grace for a group or individual, bringing a level of understanding and care into the group dynamic that simply didn't exist before. Sharing this information can also help those who tend to value one style over others to see that we all experience each of the four styles at some time. Invite participants to record the style that represents their behavior under moderate stress on their Personal Profile Puzzles.

Each person will follow the same pattern, starting from their dominant style, moving through the diagonal shift, and usually exhibiting more and more negative characteristics as stress increases. Ask participants to look at the diagram on the Stress Paths sheet for their Leadership/Interaction Style and think about their behavior under stress. Ask, "What do you do differently? Does it correspond with the pattern described?"

When we see someone operating outside of his or her style—a Dreamer who has become quiet; a Thinker who has become demanding; a Pleaser who is task-oriented; a Director who tosses his or her pen on the table and adopts a passive posture—we can offer understanding and sensitivity. Or, we can say a prayer and stay out of the way!

Fourth: Distribute the "Harmonizing the Leadership/Interaction Styles" sheet.

Make sure to provide adequate time for reading and discussing the descriptions found on pages 63-64 of ways in which we can harmonize with other styles. Invite participants to tell about experiences or stories that may illustrate these ideas. The real value of this tool is in deepening our appreciation for styles other than our own. Increasing flexibility in our interactions with others leads to deeper harmony and more effective ministry.

Collect the Personal Profile Puzzles so you can record the results on the Group Profile Grid and the PCL Summary Sheet. In closing conversation, invite comments on how various spiritual gifts influence, or are influenced by, Leadership/ Interaction Styles.

Harmonizing the Leadership/Interaction Styles

Harmonizing with Thinkers	Harmonizing with Directors
• Talk in facts and data	• Be on time
• Be on time	• Have facts at hand
• Set a slow to moderate pace	• Stay focused on task
• Allow time for questions	• Avoid chit-chat
• Use a systematic approach (agenda)	• Use clear, concise statements
• Use logic and reason	• Only make promises you will keep
• Ask for their thoughts/opinions	• Use logic
• Consider options/alternatives	• Provide limited number of options, with pros/cons for each
• Adopt a more formal manner	• Put things in writing
• Keep your voice quiet, even	• Be clear about objectives
• Don't lean forward	• Talk facts, not feelings
• Use few gestures	• Maintain eye contact
• Don't push for quick responses	• Depart quickly and graciously
• Offer periods of silence	• Don't ask too many questions
• Work with clear goals, objectives	• Don't "kiss up"
• Follow up in writing	• Don't ignore their opinions

Harmonizing with Pleasers	Harmonizing with Dreamers
• Stay calm, relaxed	• Speak with passion
• Focus on people	• Don't be too task oriented
• Speak personally, informally	• Maintain high energy level
• Respect speakers	• Be prepared to "waste" time; have some fun
• Make sure everyone is heard	• Talk in terms of "what if…?"
• Encourage expressions of doubt or concern	• Look at "big picture"
• Don't be argumentative/defensive	• Be flexible
• Minimize time pressure	• Be patient
• Invite consensus	• Tap into competitive spirit
• Offer praise/reassurance	• Talk visions, hopes, dreams
• Initiate contact; don't wait to hear from them	• Use feeling language
• Follow up	• Examine possibilities
• Be genuine and honest	• Brainstorm
• Ask what needs to be done	• Don't get baited into arguments
• Make sure everyone is clear on goals and assignments	• Don't expect minutes/agendas
	• Keep moving gently back on track

Teaching		
Tongues	0	0
Wisdom	0	5
Spiritual Gifts Cluster		
Nurturing —152	130	22
Outreaching —158	110	48
Witnessing —341	300	41
Organizing —60	60	0
Leadership/Interaction Styles		
Director	14	
Dreamer	7	
Pleaser	17	
Thinker	8	
Spirituality Web	Individual	Corporate
Head		
Heart		
Pilgrim		

Congregational Leadership: Group Profile Grid

Primary Spiritual Gift	Secondary Spiritual Gifts	Spiritual Gifts Cluster	Leadership/ Interaction Style
Giving	Helping, Administration, Knowledge	Organizing	Pleaser
Leadership	Healing, Teaching, Faith	Organizing	Director
Faith	Healing, Prophecy, Compassion	Witnessing	Thinker

LEADERSHIP/INTERACTION STYLES INTRODUCTION

Effective leaders have a keen awareness of their strengths and weaknesses. They strive to maximize their strengths and compensate for their weaknesses. Every leader operates out of one of four primary leadership styles. No one style is better or worse than any other. Understanding and managing one's dominant style is the key to effective leadership. Even more critical is the ability to identify and harmonize with the leadership styles of others with whom we work. Leadership/Interaction Styles (LIS) is a tool to help leaders identify their dominant styles and develop an appreciation of the dominant styles of others. Each of the four styles represents a combination of behaviors dealing with a person's focus (either on the task or on people) and the person's approach to ways of sharing information (either by asking or by telling). As a greater understanding of the four

styles emerges, individuals can learn to interact more effectively with one another. We no longer view other ways of acting, behaving, and thinking as right or wrong but simply view them as different. We are enabled to see the strengths of other approaches and methods that are not like our own.

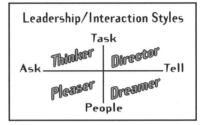

In addition, the emphasis of the LIS is not on how to change our style or alter our behavior, but instead it encourages each person to capitalize on the strengths of his or her style while minimizing the potential pitfalls due to weaknesses. It is intended to help people make the most of what they have rather than trying to make up for what they lack. Each of the four styles is effective in appropriate settings. Each is a good style. The LIS is designed to help good leaders be even better.

As we move more and more into interdependent leadership structures, such as teams, it is critically important that we find ways to interact effectively. Self-understanding is the all-important first step toward interacting well with others. The success of team-based ministry relies upon the creation of small groups of people with complementary gifts, skills, and abilities. LIS is a tool to help congregations gain information necessary to create effective leadership teams.

One last benefit of LIS: Self-perception is often quite different than the way we are perceived by others. We may feel ourselves to be a certain kind of leader, while those we work with see us in a significantly different way. Various leadership settings may call us to operate from a style that is not our predominant one. It is important to note that we will sub-optimize our leadership potential when we are cast into situations that prevent us from utilizing our dominant style. LIS can help us see where we maximize our potential and where we are forced to operate "out of our box."

DESCRIPTIVE STATEMENTS OF THE LEADERSHIP/INTERACTION STYLES

Instructions to process leader: Read the descriptions of each of the four Leadership/ Interaction Styles. Invite participants to identify themselves with the style that most accurately describes them.

Directors

Directors tend to be task oriented, focused on results and getting the job done. They stick closely to agendas, calendars, and the clock—beginning and ending at assigned times. They get down to business quickly and strive to keep everyone focused on the work to be done. They hate to waste time and are easily annoyed by side conversations and distractions. They like to be in control, and often need to be in charge. Directors often do much of their work alone rather than in groups or teams.

Directors are highly opinionated, outspoken, and decisive. They speak with authority and say exactly what they are thinking. They expect others to speak clearly and concisely, staying on topic and getting to the point quickly. They do not want or need more information than absolutely necessary to get the task accomplished. Directors are logical, linear thinkers who tend to value reason over intuition. They like very practical ideas that yield measurable, tangible results.

Directors display considerable self-confidence and are not afraid to take risks and accept responsibility for outcomes. They expect concurrence with their thinking and decisions and often do not like being challenged or corrected.

Directors are passionate and energetic about their work. Often they carry other people along with the power of their ideas and actions.

Dreamers

Dreamers tend to be sociable and people-oriented. Dreamers are committed to having a good time, and they often seem unfocused or disorganized. They are talkative, opinionated, and passionate. They maintain eye contact and may dominate a conversation. Usually, Dreamers maintain a high energy level and a great deal of enthusiasm.

Dreamers are artistic, creative, and innovative. They are able to think about many things at once. What appears to others to be a lack of concentration is for Dreamers the sign of an active mind. Dreamers focus on the big picture and often ignore details. They follow their passions and will often begin a new project before they have completed existing projects.

Dreamers are dramatic, and whatever they are interested in is all-important. They do not like being bound by rules, promises, clocks, agendas, or calendars. They prefer being spontaneous free spirits, who move wherever their hearts and minds take them.

Dreamers love a good debate and are usually persuasive in arguments. Often they think out loud—saying things they haven't fully thought through. They use many gestures when they talk (tie their hands and they can't form a complete sentence). They can often argue both sides in a debate—moving back and forth through positions until they arrive at clarity. They argue from feeling and intuition as well as reason and are sometimes annoyed by logic.

Dreamers may not keep appointments and promises, not because they are callous but because they forget to write things down and they are swept up by new thoughts, passions, and ideas.

Pleasers

Pleasers are people-oriented, often more concerned with others than with themselves. Pleasers seek to maintain balance, harmony, and civility in every setting. Pleasers try to keep everyone happy and, therefore, are often frustrated. People's needs and feelings always take precedence over tasks; therefore Pleasers are sensitive relationship builders.

Pleasers are good listeners and problem solvers. Usually diplomatic, Pleasers want to listen to all sides before coming to a conclusion. Pleasers will make sure that everyone has a chance to speak and that everyone feels they have been adequately heard. Pleasers are good at attending to group processes, emotions, and disagreements. Often, Pleasers avoid anything unpleasant, including conflict and confrontation.

Pleasers are flexible, adaptive, open to new ideas, and willing to share both responsibility and authority. Pleasers are not blamers, and they take full responsibility for problems and difficulties—even when it belongs more appropriately to someone else.

Pleasers are honest, trusting, and loyal. When they make a promise you can be sure they will keep it. They are personally sensitive and regularly get their feelings hurt. Since they do not want to hurt or distress others, they may not complain when people act inappropriately. They may silently resent not being considered or respected.

Pleasers are patient, kind, and easy to get along with. Pleasers are sometimes underestimated since they are so "nice," but their concern for justice and the general well-being makes them effective leaders.

Thinkers

Thinkers take their work seriously. A Thinker will do whatever it takes to get the job done. Highly organized, Thinkers rely on facts, information, data, and figures to make decisions. Thinkers want to gather as much information as possible, want to look at issues from as many angles as possible, and want to take as much time as needed before committing to any course of action.

Thinkers are quiet and laid-back, often withholding opinions or comments. Thinkers are cautious, and do not like making quick decisions or taking unnecessary risks. Thinkers need time to work details through in their own minds.

Thinkers prefer to have things in writing and will put things in writing for other people. Thinkers keep documentation and like to follow formal procedures and processes. Thinkers can tend to be legalistic and rigid. It is important to Thinkers that everyone pay attention, stay focused, and follow the rules. Thinkers are very much bound by calendars, agendas, timelines, blueprints, and spreadsheets. Thinkers are highly competent and exacting planners.

Thinkers often hide their own feelings and are not always attentive to the feelings of others. They may appear aloof and detached, but in reality they are most engaged when they are silent and withdrawn.

Because they attend to fine details and think through multiple scenarios, Thinkers are able to point out potential problems and obstacles. Many people perceive that Thinkers are being negative, when in reality they are trying to be prudent. Thinkers freely admit that they regularly engage in worst-case-scenario thinking, assuming that if something can go wrong, it will, but they are the first to support and defend a solid, well-designed plan. Once Thinkers make a decision, they stand behind it totally.

STRESS PATHS OF THE LEADERSHIP/INTERACTION STYLES

Confessions of a Director Under Stress—Barbara

Comfort Zone: No two ways about it, I am a **Director**: task-oriented, function best when structure and schedules are clearly defined. Don't give me too much information to process at one time. Give me a task, a checklist, and a way to chart progress and I will move mountains, one rock at a time.

1st Stress Move (diagonally across to opposite corner): If I am leading a group or working on a project with folks, and things are not going well, I will move into Pleaser mode. I will ask what people need to help get the task back on track. I will offer to help with tasks that I think are not moving quickly enough or in the *right* direction.

2nd Stress Move (vertically): If there is resistance to my *gracious* offer of help, I will move further along the stress path into

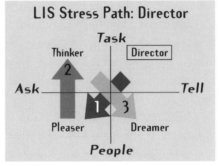

Thinker mode. I will back off from the project and reconsider options. I will brood. I will write and rewrite checklists, search for new strategies to get things moving, waiting impatiently for folks to get back in line with what I know is the right approach.

3rd Stress Move (diagonally across to opposite corner): If that doesn't work, I will move to the final stage of stress for me: Dreamer. I will throw up my hands and say, "The heck with it, and you. Do whatever you want to. If it gets done, it gets done. If not, too bad." If you see me in Dreamer mode, give me a hug or give me lots of space.

As my stress increases, and I move along to the next style, I exhibit more and more of the negative or shadow traits of that style. It is not a pretty sight when I get to Dreamer mode. Knowing what is happening does not stop it, but it does offer me perspective and an opportunity to step back from the tension and consider why I am acting in a particular way. Sometimes, that awareness is all I need to relax and operate more effectively. Eventually, it will help me be more effective when operating out of a style that is not my comfort zone.

Confessions of a Dreamer Under Stress—Dan

Comfort Zone: As a Dreamer I love ideas and debate and letting the conversation take us where it will. Nothing energizes me like a fast-paced brainstorming session or a highly interactive discussion. My competitive nature kicks in and I always enjoy "one-upping" the last idea on the table. However, when people don't listen to what I'm saying, or ignore me altogether, watch out!

1st Stress Move (diagonally across to opposite corner): When I start to feel stress, I

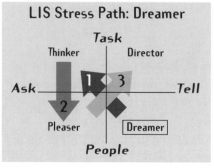

LIS Stress Path: Dreamer

withdraw to my emotional cave. I become a classic Thinker—quiet, removed, working things out in the lone recesses of my mind. Often this action is perceived as anger, but it is simply a safety net that helps me process what is going on. However, if people pursue me into my Thinker-cave, putting pressure on me to get over it, I generally back off completely, though not always gracefully.

2nd Stress Move (vertically): With the increased stress, I become a Pleaser. I will acquiesce to the majority, be pleasant (though tight-lipped), and try to make everything okay. Most people think I'm being very considerate and cooperative, and I am—but I'm also aware that my pulse is pounding and my breathing is shallow. I am just about at my limit.

3rd Stress Move (diagonally across to opposite corner): If the stress increases, I end up slamming into my extreme style, that of the Director. As a Director I exhibit few of the good qualities and almost all of the bad. I am bossy, curt, business-like, formal, and I rule with an authoritarian style. I become fixated on the task, and it is every man and woman for him- or herself. I want to get the task finished and get out!

Becoming aware of this progression has allowed me to step back from stress before it becomes too great. I look for the factors that increase stress and attempt to lessen or defuse them. I am happier with this awareness, and so are the people I work with.

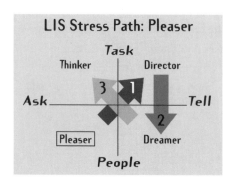

LIS Stress Path: Pleaser

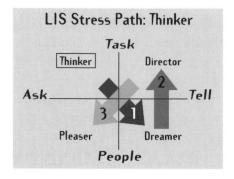

LIS Stress Path: Thinker

HARMONIZING THE LEADERSHIP/INTERACTION STYLES

While it is important to identify and understand our personal interaction styles, a greater benefit occurs as we understand the behavior styles of others. Each interaction style is characterized by a unique blend of behaviors that make perfect sense to those who possess them but are somewhat foreign, and often irritating, to those who do not. When we understand why others act as they do, and how they behave in a variety of social settings, we are able to be more accepting, more flexible, and more effective ourselves. Groups that accomplish the most tend to harmonize a variety of behavioral styles. Here are some helpful insights in how to harmonize with each leadership/interaction style.

Harmonizing With Directors

When dealing with Directors, remember how much they value punctuality, structure, and order. Have your facts at hand and don't spend too much time on small talk. Stay focused and make sure that you make clear, concise statements. Directors appreciate honesty, eye contact, and clarifying questions. Directors expect people to accomplish the defined task and to be logical, practical, and efficient. Directors don't like argument or debate, but they honor well-reasoned, balanced opinion.

Harmonizing With Dreamers

When working with Dreamers, stay flexible and tolerant. Dreamers see deadlines and rules as restrictive. Dreamers love to talk about ideas, and they need people to look at many different options. Getting along with Dreamers requires the ability to talk feelings as well as thinking, dreams as well as goals, and "what if" as well as "what is." Dreamers lose interest if the passion and energy levels drop too low, and they need to argue and debate ideas to fully grasp and understand them. Just because Dreamers don't produce agendas, minutes, policies, and procedures doesn't mean that they are lazy, careless, or poor leaders. Dreamers manage huge amounts of information and ideas in their heads. The extra time spent helping to retrieve what Dreamers know is well worth the effort.

Harmonizing With Pleasers

Pleasers are the easiest people in the world to get along with. Pleasers work best with those who maintain an even temper and a balanced perspective. Don't argue or raise your voice. Be clear with instructions and expectations. Don't pull surprises or expect Pleasers to read your mind. Pleasers will do everything in their power to keep peace and to maintain the status quo. They will do just about anything that is asked of them, but will only resent it when they feel taken advantage of. Pleasers want to make sure everyone is included and listened to. Give Pleasers enough time to make sure that all the details are covered and that they understand what is expected. Pleasers thrive when there is lots of free-flowing communication and follow-up.

63

Harmonizing With Thinkers

Patience is more than a virtue when dealing with Thinkers—it is essential. Thinkers need time and space to explore all options. They want as much information to process as possible before making any decisions. Don't push them for answers, and be able to explain why any risky decision is a good idea. Work silence into your process, and take time periodically to review decisions that have been made. Follow formal procedures and establish clear boundaries. Where appropriate, document work on paper. Provide as much information to Thinkers as you can prior to meetings or to the time when they are required to make decisions.

Each and every behavior style is a gift. The ways we interact with others are incomplete in and of themselves. We need one another. When we understand why other people behave differently than we do, we are able to reduce the stress and tension in almost any group process. Thereby we make our own lives easier and more painless.

LEADERSHIP/INTERACTION STYLES: INTERPRETIVE HELPS

Remember: Every person can and does operate out of all four Leadership/Interaction Styles depending on the setting and need, but there tends to be a predominant style for each person.

Directors

Positives—Directors get things done, and they seldom get sidetracked. Forming a vision is never a problem because everyone has one and no one is afraid to share it. Most Directors develop good management skills, and they delegate responsibility. No one needs to keep an eye on Directors—they do a good job of keeping promises, meeting deadlines, and completing tasks. Directors stay focused and they attend to all the details. They are great at chairing committees and designing processes.

Potential Negatives—When Directors are too task-oriented, people can get lost. Directors tend to neglect relationship building when there is a job to do. Also, program can become so important that fellowship is lost. Directors are not always the best listeners. When there are too many Directors with their own clarity of vision, they often move in many different directions, and then nothing of value gets accomplished.

Implications of a High Director Concentration—This makeup could indicate that the congregation has attracted Directors and gives them the kind of freedom they need to keep them happy. It could also indicate that there is such emphasis on task in the church that Dreamers and Pleasers are operating under stress, and therefore are forced to operate out of their boxes. (Under stress, we swing to our opposite corner: Pleasers become Directors under stress; Thinkers become Dreamers; Directors become Pleasers; and Dreamers become Thinkers. When two types dominate, they operate within their comfort range, and can force the other two types to function under stress, thus creating a skewed distribution.) Making things happen should be no problem. Keeping people happy about what is happening might be more of a challenge. Channeling all of the energy and leadership toward a common mission and aim may be all but impossible. Also, new vision may be limited since vision tends to come from the Dreamers. This means that innovation may be slower in coming in congregations dominated by Directors. Pleasers make sure that people don't get run over by process. Who owns that responsibility when Pleasers are absent? Director leadership may result in a church that is "program rich" but "relationship poor."

Dreamers

Positives—Dreamers see possibilities, and they are fearless when it comes to trying new ideas. They are fun, and they remember to keep things in perspective. Dreamers are creative, and they often see many solutions to a single problem. They are unstoppable, and they seldom give up once they start something. Dreamers are community builders, and they hold the centrality of fellowship sacred. They don't take no for an answer, and they look for new ways to do things all the time.

Potential Negatives—Dreamers don't always know their limitations, and they sometimes overcommit. Dreamers jump horses at midstream because they tend to focus where their passion is currently burning. They can appear undependable and undermine trust. Dreamers get so wrapped up in people that they lose sight of task. Often, Dreamers have problems seeing things from other points of view. Dreamers can be totally unaware that things are headed in a wrong direction until it is too late to change course.

Implications of a High Dreamer Concentration—Where Dreamers prevail, there is always a great deal of creativity, innovation, and energy. Very little becomes stale or boring in Dreamer congregations.

Conversely, many times nothing gets finished; Dreamers are great at start-up but lousy at follow-through. Organizational skills are scarce, and the ability to set reasonable goals and meet deadlines is low at best. Dreamer congregations are so fixated on the big picture that they often miss critical details.

Another drawback reported by many Dreamer-heavy churches is the amount of animosity and conflict that arises. Artistic, creative, passionate people may be narrow in their openness to ideas not their own. Turf wars can erupt as individuals attempt to gain support for their new ideas. So many good ideas can compete for attention that resources are spread too thin.

Dreamer congregations show enormous potential that they rarely live up to. Dreamers are the quickest to get frustrated with their situation and leave the church for other congregations and opportunities to serve.

Pleasers

Positives—Pleasers are the diplomats. They focus on maintaining good interpersonal dynamics within the group. They balance task with people. They look to the needs of the whole rather than the parts. Pleasers are servant leaders who create balanced, comfortable environments for work and play. Pleasers tend to be broadly focused and invite the input of many. Pleasers are inclusive and extremely flexible. Pleasers are easy to work for, work with, and work around.

Potential Negatives—Pleasers are not task oriented and can seem ineffective. Pleasers do not tend to be visionary leaders, and they can expend a lot of time maintaining the status quo. Pleasers are slower by nature and can make processes grind to a halt. Pleasers can be overly sensitive, and they often hold grudges that make it hard to work with them in the future. Pleasers often are less than honest in an effort not to hurt feelings, and they do not hold people accountable or delegate responsibility for fear of insulting others.

Implications of a High Pleaser Concentration—Pleaser is the predominant style in The United Methodist Church. The image of a Pleaser-dominated church is that it is a nice place to be. Interactions are marked by civility, reason, pleasant conversation, and a real concern for feelings, thoughts, and needs of others. Issues generally are thoroughly discussed, everyone has a chance to be heard, and listening at the deep levels actually occurs.

Underlying the niceness, however, can be a real frustration. Often Pleasers acquiesce to things they are not truly in support of in order not to make waves. Real feelings are left unspoken, or they are spoken privately (but rarely to the person they concern). As stress builds, Pleasers become Directors. They tend to become lone rangers, doing things themselves rather than enlisting the aid of others ("I'd rather do it myself!"). Often Pleasers get their feelings hurt when others don't get as excited about their ideas as they do.

Pleasers also report that they feel like they work all the time but nothing ever gets done. The more they do, the more there is left to do. Because Pleasers are so agreeable, they often get called on to do more and more. Pleasers are not well versed in the art of saying no.

A heavy concentration of Pleasers often means that the congregation is in recovery from an unpleasant experience. Where unresolved conflict exists, church people often revert to a nice, civil attitude. This attitude may mask a variety of feelings. Where are the creativity (Dreamer), direction (Director), and strategic planning (Thinker) responsibilities lodged in a Pleaser-based congregation? How can the leadership broaden their styles to be more inclusive?

Thinkers

Positives—Thinkers are detail masters, and they make sure that things get done. They are seldom pushy but often persuasive. Thinkers cover all the bases, and often see things that others miss. Thinkers listen effectively, and process great amounts of information. They tend to have good memories, and they are knowledgeable about many things. Thinkers are cautious, and they work through problems that stump other styles of leadership. They stay focused, clear about the task, and they don't get easily distracted.

Potential Negatives—Thinkers can be slow and unwilling to try new things. They may become so focused on task that relationships suffer. Many Thinkers are lone rangers, and they don't connect in fellowship. Thinkers are indecisive unless they have a Director or a Dreamer bugging them to hurry up. Thinkers tend to withhold information, and they can sometimes torpedo programs by a rigid adherence to the rules.

Implications of a High Thinker Concentration—We can only speculate on what a Thinker-dominated congregation might look like. In working with approximately two hundred different congregations, there has never been one dominated by Thinkers. The most obvious reason may be that where Thinkers ruled, nothing would ever happen, different camps would form, and over time there would be nothing attractive to outsiders.

Thinkers provide valuable perspective and wisdom to any congregation, but they are the most passive, pensive, and cautious of the four styles. They are quiet, slow, and stubborn—with all the good and bad each quality provides.

Ultimately, the Thinker style illustrates graphically why no one style is healthy, nor adequate upon which to build a leadership base. We need balance, and where balance does not exist, we need understanding of all four types to provide appropriate correctives.

CHAPTER 4

Spirituality Web

INSTRUCTIONS FOR THE GROUP LEADER
Download Handouts and Group Process Materials from
www.equippedforeverygoodwork.org

This third tool—the Spirituality Web—provides still another dimension to the discovery and appreciation of the ways in which a group or church is uniquely equipped to do God's work. As you work through the tool, encourage use of the Spiritual Gifts Inventory and the Leadership/Interaction Styles as aids in understanding the Spirituality Types. The Spirituality Web is designed and intended to facilitate dialogue and exploration in a group setting. Try to provide adequate time for responses after each category is completed. It is in conversation that discovery and understanding will happen—in the spaces between the outlined steps.

First: Return the Personal Profile Puzzles and distribute the Individual Spirituality Web sheets.

Tell the group about the history and development of the Spirituality Web (using the Spirituality Web Introduction on page 73; also available on the website). This information relates the Spirituality Types to the Spiritual Gifts and provides an understanding of the value this exercise offers the group.

MATERIALS
pencils

writing surface
(table groupings are best)

GROUP PROCESS MATERIALS
Personal Profile Puzzle

PCL Summary Sheet: Putting the Pieces Together

PCL: Group Profile Grid

HANDOUTS
Spirituality Web Introduction

Spirituality Web Worksheets: Individual and Corporate

Spirituality Web Lists: Individual and Corporate

Means of Grace Webs

Second: Make sure names are recorded in the center of each person's individual Spirituality Web. Read through the Individual Spirituality Web List (on page 74; also available on the website) for each Spirituality Type, inviting participants to make a notation on their web if they respond strongly, either positively or negatively, to a particular type.

Note: As a leader, here is an opportunity for you to apply your new knowledge of the Leadership/Interaction Styles. Directors and Dreamers will not need more than an instruction to write a response in the appropriate space. They will decide where and what form that response should take. Director responses will be orderly and neat. Dreamer responses may be pictures, upside-down, or not written down at all. Pleasers will want to know what kind of response you want to see. Thinkers will see benefit in having some explicit system of response for each category. If you provide one, it is very likely that Pleasers will use it too.

Third: Distribute copies of the Means of Grace Webs (available from the website).

As you describe each of the Spirituality Types through the lens of the means of grace, using the "Descriptive Statements on Spirituality Types" (found on pages 75-79), the participants should record, on their Individual Webs (not the Means of Grace Webs), the name of the means of grace (prayer, study, Lord's Supper, fasting, Christian conference, acts of mercy) under the Spirituality Type that best reflects their most meaningful experience of that discipline and that feels like the best fit.

Remind them that this is not about what we wish we experienced or what we believe we ought to experience, but what most accurately reflects who and where we are now in our spiritual relationship with God. Encourage the participants to listen to the entire list for a means of grace before responding. Repeat information, if necessary.

Take, for example, "Prayer," the first means of grace listed. As you read about the six Spirituality Types in relation to prayer, a participant who responds strongly to the description of the Mystic approach and experience of prayer should write *prayer* in the "Mystic" space on her or his Web. Someone else may respond strongly to both Heart and Pilgrim. This person should write *prayer* in both "Heart" and "Pilgrim" spaces on his or her Web.

Spirituality Web: Individual

Crusader   Head

Servant
Name _____   Heart
            Prayer

Mystic   Pilgrim
        Prayer

When you have finished all of the means of grace descriptions, each person will have a composite picture of his or her own Web of Spirituality. Usually, one type will dominate the picture, but the means of grace listings may be distributed across three or four types. There is no right or wrong here. What's important is the increase in understanding of ourselves and others. Have participants record the Spirituality Type they identify with most strongly on their Personal Profile Puzzle and circle it on their Web.

Fourth: Invite participants with the same Primary Spiritual Gift to compare their responses to various categories. Or, use the Spiritual Gift listed most often in the group and discuss how the six Spirituality Types would express that gift. Begin to build appreciation for the different ways we live out of our gifts.

Let's look at Evangelism as an example. Keep in mind that not one of these examples requires an individual to serve on a committee or commission of Evangelism. Spiritual gifts are lived out through our spirituality wherever we find ourselves.

Head Evangelism: Organize a study program and prepare handouts.
Heart Evangelism: Share your faith story in one-on-one sharing or worship testimony.
Pilgrim Evangelism: Share questions with other seekers.
Mystic Evangelism: Listen one-on-one to the stories of others.
Servant Evangelism: Witness to Christ's love by example.
Crusader Evangelism: Speak in a stadium event.

Fifth: Distribute the Corporate Spirituality Webs.

Each individual should write his or her own name in the center of the corporate web. Read through the Corporate Spirituality Type Lists (pages 80-81). Then repeat the means of grace statements used earlier (pages 75-79). As before, invite participants to listen and record their responses, but this time, they are presenting their perception of which

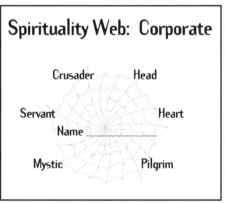

Spirituality Type is most reflected in the way the church practices each of the means of grace. For instance, participants who feel that this congregation performs acts of mercy in the manner described for Head spirituality will write *acts of mercy* in the space under "Head." When the process is complete, each person will have a composite picture of his or her view of the corporate spirituality.

Invite the participants to record their impressions of the dominant Spirituality Type of the group or congregation on their Personal Profile Puzzles. Collect the puzzles so that you can record the individual and corporate responses on the Group Profile Grid and the PCL Summary Sheet. Remember to note patterns and anomalies for further discussion.

roup Profile Grid					Primary	Secondary
					3	12
					0	1
Spiritual Gifts Cluster	Leadership/ Interaction Style	Spirituality Type Individual	Spirituality Type Corporate	Task	2	7
					0	6
					0	5
					0	4
					13	22
Organizing	Pleaser	Pilgrim	Head		3	7
					11	19
					4	10
					0	2
					2	12
Organizing	Director	Head	Head		1	7
					3	15
					1	10
					1	14
					0	1
Witnessing	Thinker	Servant	Heart		6	8
					0	0
					0	5
					130	22
					110	48
					300	41
					60	0

Outreaching	—158	
Witnessing	—341	
Organizing	—60	
Leadership/Interaction Styles		
Director		14
Dreamer		7
Pleaser		17
Thinker		8
Spirituality Web	Individual	Corporate
Head	7	27
Heart	24	18
Pilgrim	10	3
Mystic	5	2
Servant	6	6
Crusader	1	0
Task Types		
Project		
Work		

Use the discussion questions below to continue the dialogue, perhaps in small groups or in one-on-one sharing. If you plan to split into small groups, first have the larger group reflect on these two questions:

1. How and where does the church provide (or not provide) opportunities for each of the different Spirituality Types to encounter God?
2. What are the similarities and differences between the individual types represented in the group and the group's perception of the overall corporate, or church, type?

For small-group discussions, put people with the same Primary Gift together to concentrate on understanding how the Spirituality Types influence how we live out of our gifts. Another approach is to make sure there is a good mix of Gifts and Types within each group. This mixing will deepen appreciation of the dimensions of giftedness. Invite small groups to share their insights with the larger group after a time of discussion.

Small-Group Discussion Questions
- How well does the Spirituality Type of my church fit with my Spirituality Type?
- What is the best way for me to develop my spiritual life?
- Why is my expression of spirituality different from that of others?
- How do others see our church (or group)?
- What does this say about our ability to reach out to the community?
- How can we enrich experience for those whose needs are not being met?
- What are we doing right?

72

SPIRITUALITY WEB INTRODUCTION

We are each gifted by the Spirit to do the work of ministry best suited to who we are and to our deep passions. We understand that it is only in linking our gifts that their true value and power are employed. If each community of faith were made up of twenty individuals, with all twenty gifts represented, that would be a good foundation from which to do ministry. But in our churches there will be several people with the same gifts but not the same interests or ways of doing things. The process of gifts discovery does not stop with naming and defining our gifts. We need to look further to really begin to know and grow with one another.

We are all in the same circle of faith but have individual ways of living and moving within the circle. The choices we make about how we deepen our relationship with God and live out our stewardship of God's gifts make each person's journey unique.

In his book *A History of Christian Spirituality*, Urban T. Holmes provides a spiritual typology that describes the different ways we approach and experience God. Holmes started with four types and later added a fifth, and we have recently recognized the need for a sixth.[1] All are represented on the Spirituality Web. Each represents a combination of the vertical axis of Approach and the horizontal axis of Experience. Approach, to use the image of a radio, refers to the ways we transmit to God; Experience refers to the ways we receive from God.

Approach/Experience Grid

The life of Jesus provides a model for integration of all types. He moved easily between solitude and community, study and action, praise and silence. We all experience all six types, and each has value, but one type tends to dominate for each of us. The community of faith requires individuals of each type and of all types. As with spiritual gifts, identifying our dominant type helps us know ourselves and each other and appreciate and respect our differences. In addition, studying ways we can cultivate and grow toward areas of experience and approach that are foreign to us helps us move toward integration, balance, and wholeness. The need for this integration can be underscored by a widely quoted statement by Abraham Maslow that a person with no tool except a hammer begins to treat everything like a nail.

Combined with our new knowledge about our spiritual gifts, the Spirituality Types provide an added dimension, a more detailed map or picture for understanding and developing our gifts in ways uniquely suited to who we are.

SPIRITUALITY WEB LIST (INDIVIDUAL)

Head Spirituality
- Study of Scripture is central
- Worship and education define church
- God can be known
- Faith is rational
- The Christian life has practical benefits

Heart Spirituality
- Focus is on relationship with Jesus
- Faith sharing is essential
- There is a strong commitment to prayer for others
- Experience rather than study is preferred for knowing God
- There is a praise orientation

Pilgrim Spirituality
- A person seeks meaning
- A person looks for answers
- There is openness to a wide variety of faith traditions
- A person accepts what makes sense
- Faith formation is a process—a journey

Mystic Spirituality
- Focus is on the mystery of God
- Prayer and meditation are central
- Retreat/renewal is important
- God is listened for
- Personal spiritual development is goal

Servant Spirituality
- People should be doers, not hearers
- Outlook is anti-institutional
- God is unknowable
- Christianity means being like Jesus
- Golden Rule and Great Commandment define faith
- Prayer is secondary

Crusader Spirituality
- A person feels single-minded devotion to call
- All time, energy, and resources are committed to success
- Spiritual discipline provides focus
- Christian community is found with like-minded Crusaders

DESCRIPTIVE STATEMENTS ON SPIRITUALITY TYPES
Encountering God Through the Means of Grace

PRAYER

Head

Head prayer is *formal* and based in *words*, often in written form. The reason for prayer is to attain a deeper *understanding* of God and what God requires.

Heart

Heart prayer is *informal* and spontaneous. In prayer I am *asking* God to participate in my life or in the lives of others. Intercessory prayer is a popular form of Heart prayer. The reason for prayer is to deepen my *relationship* with God and others.

Pilgrim

Pilgrim prayer is a *seeking* for God. "Where, who, what are you, God?" Filled with *questions*, Pilgrims pray as part of their ongoing search for *meaning*.

Mystic

Mystic prayer is characterized by *silence*. The twenty-second moment of silence observed in many churches is a source of deep frustration for Mystics. In order to truly *listen* for God within, a much longer period of time is required and can take many hours. The aim of Mystic prayer is *union* with Christ.

Servant

Servant prayer is characterized by the statement "My life is my prayer." Prayer is *action*-based, providing an *example* of Christian witness in the world. Through prayer, Servants seek *guidance* in the work to which they are called.

Crusader

Crusader prayer is for *strength* to stay the course. Their prayer is deeply *focused* on their cause. The reason for prayer is to move ever closer to *victory!*

STUDY OF SCRIPTURE

Head

For Head spirituality, study is a means of gathering *information*. It is a *scholarly* pursuit, undertaken in a search for deeper *knowledge* of God and God's will.

Heart

There is *inspiration* in every story of the biblical witness for Heart spirituality. "Tell me the stories of Jesus I long to hear." The *anecdotal*, or storytelling, focus of study for Heart spirituality provides *guidance* for living a life of true faith in relationship with God and others.

Pilgrim

Pilgrims study for *instruction* in the doctrines, practices, and theology of the faith. The study itself is an important *experience* and will only be truly beneficial if there is room for interaction. Pilgrims will ask lots of questions in a study group. Pilgrims study to gain deeper *understanding* of who and what God is, and what that means in the life of faith. Surprising to some, DISCIPLE Bible study has revealed latent Pilgrims who have been pillars in the church for decades.

Mystic

Reflection on the *revelation* of the divine in the Scriptures is the approach to study for Mystics. It is an act of *devotion* and will often be undertaken in private, with a mixture of reading and meditation.

Servant

When Servants study Scripture, it is something like looking at the instruction manual. What *directions* are offered? Where is the life of service *modeled* in the Scriptures? Study provides *encouragement* for Servants and examples to encourage others in their lives of service.

Crusader

Crusaders know that their cause is the right one. They study to find *reinforcement* for their *vision* reflected in the Scriptures. Their study will be *focused* in those areas that support their work.

LORD'S SUPPER

Head

For Head spirituality, the *ritual* of the Lord's Supper is most important. These people will be comfortable following the same *liturgical* form each time. The Great Thanksgiving in *The United Methodist Hymnal* is a Head liturgy for Communion. The *discipline* of partaking in the ritual of Communion is the reason for Communion.

Heart

For Heart spirituality, Communion is a *celebration* of the relationship with Jesus. That celebration may be joyful or filled with sorrow, but it will always be *emotional.* The act of Communion provides a personal *connection* with the life and suffering of Jesus.

Pilgrim

Pilgrims will *explore* Communion. It is a journey of *discovery* into the experience itself in hopes of *expanding* understanding of meaning and purpose.

Mystic

The spiritual discipline of Communion is a *personal* act of *devotion* for Mystics. Through the mystery and sacred nature of the Eucharist, Mystics seek *union with the Christ.*

Servant

For Servant spirituality, as for Head spirituality, the Lord's Supper is important as *ritual.* But unlike people with Head spirituality, Servants participating in Communion are *empowered* by *connection* with Jesus, the suffering servant. Heart spirituality celebrates Communion in order to connect. Servants connect through Communion in order to be empowered.

Crusader

Crusaders *identify* with the life and suffering of Christ. Communion is a *consecration* of their struggles and cause and provides nourishment and *strength* for the work.

FASTING/ABSTINENCE

Head

The *ritual* of fasting is an important spiritual discipline, an act of obedience to God's will as recorded in the Scriptures. It is a required *task* and there is great reward in its *accomplishment*.

Heart

Fasting is an act of *devotion* for Heart spirituality. It is *focused* through the feelings and senses. The experience of fasting brings a deep sense of *holiness*.

Pilgrim

For Pilgrims, fasting is a way of experiencing *clarity*. The Pilgrim will *empty* himself or herself in order to know what the experience itself brings and perhaps to find *new direction* for the quest.

Mystic

For Mystics, too, fasting is a way of experiencing *clarity*. But rather than emptying, like Pilgrims, Mystics *open* through fasting to the presence of the holy within, *centering* body, mind, and spirit on the deeper life.

Servant

Fasting for Servants is an act of *compassion*. The fast is *inspiring* to Servants and the community they serve. It is a means of expressing *solidarity* with the suffering of those in need.

Crusader

Fasting is a *political* statement for Crusaders (think Dick Gregory or Gandhi). It is an act of *confirmation* that their cause is just and provides *renewed inner strength* for the journey toward fulfillment of the vision.

CHRISTIAN CONFERENCE
(Christian Conversation, True Fellowship)

Head

For Head spirituality, talking with other Christians is a means of *sharing knowledge*. The *formal* structure of the class meeting would be a comfortable setting for Head spirituality. The reason for such conference is to promote a clear *understanding* of God's will and how to be more obedient to God's will.

Heart

Phone chats during the week, the coffee hour after worship—these are Heart domains for Christian conference. The joy and *fellowship* of *informal* conversations are a means to deepening *relationship* with God through relationships with other Christians.

Pilgrim

For Pilgrims, every conversation is an *exploration* into the life of faith. Sometimes, the coffee hour can be an effective forum for these conversations as well. Pilgrims will have lots of questions and will relish the *interpersonal* nature of true conversation. Such fellowship is always in service to *expanding* understanding of meaning and purpose in one's own life and in the lives of others.

Mystic

Christian conference for Mystics is a *devotional* act. It will most likely occur *one-on-one*. For Mystics, large groups cannot adequately focus on the presence within. Again, *union* with Christ through the revelation of Godself in others is the reason for such conversations.

Servant

Servants engage in Christian conversation to gain *strength* for the work before them. They are seeking *support* from the group or individual, and the talk will be *topical*, focused on the work at hand.

Crusader

Crusaders talk to others in order to rally *support for the cause.* A conversation is a Christian conference if it is a *recruiting* opportunity, *focused* closely on the cause.

ACTS OF MERCY

Head

For Head spirituality, these acts will be *organized* and planned. The Lord *requires* that we act justly. Acts of mercy are part of our obedience to God's will. The meaning of the act comes from its satisfactory *accomplishment.*

Heart

Heart spirituality motivates people to engage in acts of mercy out of *compassion* for others. It is important to engage face-to-face, to build *relationships* with those served. One serves others because it is *pleasing to God.* In contrast to Head spirituality, in which such acts are what God requires, in Heart spirituality they are what God wants.

Pilgrim

Pilgrims are seekers with a basic will to do good. Random acts of kindness may often characterize the acts of mercy of the Pilgrim spirituality. *Caring* for others and *doing good,* in small and large ways, will occur spontaneously. The important thing is that such acts be *relevant* to the life of the Pilgrim.

Mystic

For Mystics, acts of mercy connect them with the *divine spark* in the world. They will engage in such acts on a *small scale.* The benefit of this means of grace for Mystics is the *balance* it provides. Occasional connection with the world and its needs is essential in maintaining a healthy life of faith.

Servant

For Servants, acts of mercy are a way of life. Servants are *energized* through serving the needs of others, and they derive deep *satisfaction* in *obedience* to God's call to action.

Crusader

Crusaders engage in acts of mercy that *support their vision.* If it will *build momentum* for their cause, they will do it. The reason for such acts is to *inspire others* to join them in this critical work.

Spirituality Web List (Corporate)

Head Spirituality
- Focus is on theology
- Worship is liturgical
- Emphasis is on education
- Worship follows set patterns
- There is a need for right answers
- Preaching is important

Heart Spirituality
- Fellowship is important
- Worship is festive, emotional
- Singing is important
- Prayer is corporate and spoken
- Emphasis is on evangelism, conversion

Pilgrim Spirituality
- There is openness to questions
- Worship and activities are highly interactive
- Community is small-group based
- Worship is highly experiential
- Focus is on relevance to daily living
- Belief and action are closely linked

Mystic Spirituality
- Outlook is contemplative
- There is focus on discipline
- Silence is more important than sound (preaching/singing)
- Worship is liturgical
- There is focus on inward spiritual formation
- Writing is important

Spirituality Web

Servant Spirituality

- Faith is action
- Service is critical
- We serve the God in others
- Works define community
- Church is in the world
- There is clarity of purpose

Crusader Spirituality

- Focus is on task
- All resources are geared toward task
- Everyone is in agreement on task
- Faith equals commitment to task
- Distractions are not tolerated

SPIRITUALITY WEB: INTERPRETIVE HELPS

The six types of spirituality represent different ways that we encounter God. Our relationship with God includes both the way we approach God and the way we experience God.

Evidence is strong that the vast majority of newcomers to United Methodist congregations are either Heart or Pilgrim spiritualities.

Questions

- What ongoing experiences do we provide to encourage the participation of underrepresented spiritualities?
- How can we broaden what we already do without alienating the predominant spiritualities?
- How can we add new experiences that allow for a variety of spiritualities?

Head Spirituality

Head spirituality is the predominant type of spirituality in United Methodist congregations. We have worked long and hard to create a Head church—we have a Head hymnal, a Head *Book of Worship*, a Head *Book of Discipline*, Head studies like DISCIPLE, and Head support systems like charge conferences. There is nothing wrong with Head spirituality. It is not bad! It simply is not the only authentic approach to God, and we hurt our commitment to inclusiveness when we are unaware of how solidly Head-type we have become as a denomination.

The only time a Head approach poses a problem is when it is our predominant congregational style but is out of sync with the majority of individual styles in the congregation.

- In what ways are we Head-type out of habit? In what ways are we Head-type by choice?
- What alternatives do we offer people to a Head-type worship experience? What about our congregational worship style appeals to other Spirituality Types? (Ask them.)
- What are the predominant Spirituality Types of the people currently responsible for planning/conducting worship? How do they feel about our worship experience on Sunday morning?

Heart Spirituality

United Methodism has been infused by many different faith communions in the past generation. Many of them are evangelical and focused inward. Culturally, people are seeking two benefits from church association: (1) strengthening of a personal (pietistic) faith, and (2) community. Surveys report that the vast majority of United Methodist worshipers are seeking joy, inspiration, comfort, and connection in worship. The number one reason given for defection from The United Methodist Church is "uninspiring worship." Head-type worship is considered dry and unspiritual by Heart spiritualities.

- What worshiping experiences do we offer that are designed for the spiritual formation needs of Heart believers?
- In what ways is our preaching: informational (teaching), formational (shepherding), transformational (prophetic/invitational)?
- What opportunities are given throughout the ministry of the church for members to tell their faith stories to one another?

Pilgrim Spirituality

Urban Holmes never talked about a Pilgrim category, but this category is the fastest-growing segment of The United Methodist Church. More people come into our churches from other faith traditions than come in through profession of faith and baptism.

People are looking for a spirituality that will make sense and that will meet them where they are. Pilgrims do not want to be told what to believe, but they want safe places to explore what a faith has to offer. They are willing to draw the best from a variety of sources, and sometimes end up with a pastiche religion—a religion with many unmatched pieces.

Churches need to see Pilgrims as an opportunity to learn rather than a problem to solve. Pilgrims do not need to be corrected or fixed. They need to be in relationship with people who can offer them a new perspective.

- How do we relate to newcomers who question the status quo?
- How would people feel about someone who interrupted the preacher during a sermon to ask questions?
- How would members of the church respond to someone who quoted Buddha, Mohammed, and Confucius as often as he or she quoted Jesus?
- How well would someone new to the Christian faith understand what happens during morning worship?
- Who is responsible to welcome and guide newcomers into the church?
- What are the forums for questioning and seeking currently available to both members and nonmembers?

Mystic Spirituality

In United Methodism, Mystic spirituality is the lost prodigal. The United Methodist Church has never owned the mystical tradition as its own in America. Most Methodist Mystics have departed for greener pastures in the past. One comment from a Mystic is that United Methodist worship makes Mystics nervous and restless the minute the organ begins to play. This kind of worship is a painful experience for a Mystic. Mystics are good at martyrdom, but there must be something that feeds them in order to keep them around.

Many United Methodist churches are lacking in spiritual life and regular centering. All too often, spiritual growth and discipline is turned into a task or a program of the church. We need more Mystics in leadership who can calm us, center us, and direct us. Listen to the Mystics. Ask what they see, ask what they seek, ask what they think the church is lacking.

- Where can Mystics find nurture and feeding in our church?
- Are there worshiping alternatives that provide silence, space, devotional guidance, and shared prayer?

Servant Spirituality

Servant spirituality is quickly emerging as a force to be reckoned with in Methodism. Doers can tolerate a Head worship experience, as long as there are adequate opportunities to serve and work, both within and outside the congregation. Resistance to Servant spirituality revolves around a basic sense that for Servants the church is a means to an end rather than an end in itself. Servants are much more likely to go where the action is: their loyalty is to Christ first, to the ministry second, and lastly to a local congregation. They are the least patient, the most volatile, and the hardest of the spiritualities to deter.

- Are Servants encouraged to go ahead and do things in our church?
- Do formal structures ever prevent Servants from engaging in meaningful ministry?
- Servants prefer doing to planning. Are they suffering in our church by sitting on committees that they feel waste time? (Ask them.) Is the work they do on committees fulfilling to them?

Crusader Spirituality

Urban Holmes once lumped highly-committed individuals into the category of fanatic. Later in his life, he realized that some people are simply so committed to their sense of call and vision that they will sacrifice everything to be faithful.[2]

Crusaders are rare, and they often leave the organized church because there is very little support for their zeal. Crusaders find that it is easier to gather like-minded, similarly committed people to their cause, and a large organization slows them down. However, many Crusaders get their launch from a community of faith.

- What does our church do to help people discern call and vision?
- When people are convinced that God is calling them to some specialized ministry, how does our leadership respond?
- How willing is the church to launch individuals into the world to serve in mission and ministry?
- What processes are available to people for seeking understanding of God's will for their lives—both individually and corporately?

NOTES

1. See *A History of Christian Spirituality: An Analytical Introduction,* by Urban T. Holmes (Seabury Press, 1980). Holmes expanded his ideas in lectures during a seminar course in Muncie, Indiana, in 1983.

2. See *A History of Christian Spirituality: An Analytical Introduction,* by Urban T. Holmes (Seabury Press, 1980). Holmes expanded these ideas as well during his 1983 lectures in a seminar course in Muncie, Indiana.

CHAPTER 5

Task Type Preferences

INSTRUCTIONS FOR THE GROUP LEADER
Download Handouts and Group Process Materials from
www.equippedforeverygoodwork.org

The final piece of the puzzle is Task Type Preferences. Spiritual Gifts and Spirituality Types focus on our relationship with God and our spiritual links to one another. Leadership/Interaction Styles help us see how our behavior influences those relationships. The Task Type Preferences Survey explores four ways to gather together to do the work for which we are equipped. When the groups in which we work are structured in ways we enjoy, we are happier and more effective.

Interviews were held with hundreds of United Methodist congregations to determine their most effective working situations. From the mass of data emerged a recurrent pattern of four key motivations people named to explain why they joined working groups. Most people join a working group that has a clearly defined purpose, where they participate from start to finish—planning, organizing, implementing, and evaluating. These people make up the Project group category. Many people join groups in the Fellowship category. They want to accomplish the goals of the group, but being with other like-minded people is of the utmost importance. A smaller portion of the population enjoys groups that focus on the accomplishment of a specific task that requires a short time frame and specialized skill.

MATERIALS
pencils

writing surface
(table groupings are best)

GROUP PROCESS MATERIALS
Personal Profile Puzzle

PCL Summary Sheet:
Putting the Pieces Together

PCL: Group Profile Grid

HANDOUTS
Task Type Preferences
Survey

Task Type Descriptions

These people form the Work group. Lastly, a few people enjoy joining ongoing projects and programs to make decisions and focus on planning. This Process group usually doesn't initiate new programs but instead monitors and maintains what already exists.

There is a current movement toward team-based ministry. Of the four working groups, only the Project group represents a true team. Our working definition of *team* is "a small number of people with complementary skills who are committed to a common purpose, performance goals, and approach for which they hold themselves mutually accountable."[1] Fellowship groups and Work groups generally carry out tasks defined by other working groups such as Project and Process groups. Process groups most closely resemble the current committee structure used by the majority of United Methodist churches, though it is the least popular and least effective of the four preferred Task Types.

In every instance, people report that they are most effective, efficient, and engaged when they are allowed to interact in the work setting they prefer. People burn out and get frustrated when they are placed in situations that they do not enjoy. The tendency in our churches is to ignore these preferences and place the majority of our best people in Process settings. We should make our working policies and procedures reflect the Task Type preferences of the people instead of making people adapt to established policies and procedures. We might find a greater number of people willing to take part in leadership were we to honor their preferences. The Task Type Preferences Survey allows the congregation to explore the four different working group styles.

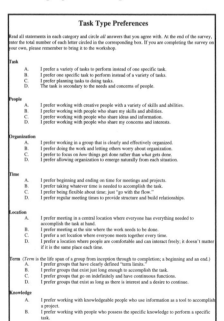

First: Distribute the Task Type Preferences Surveys and the Personal Profile Puzzles. Read through the instructions with the group to insure that everyone understands them. You may either read the statements aloud or give the group 15–20 minutes to complete the survey on their own.

Second: When everyone has had time to complete the survey, have them total and record their responses on their surveys. Reveal the names of the four types:

A. Project   C. Process

B. Work   D. Fellowship

Have people record the name of their dominant Task Type on their Personal Profile Puzzles. Count group totals for each Task Type by a show of hands and note these for reflection during the discussion.

88

Third: Read through the Task Type Descriptions (found on page 90 and on the website). Relate the descriptions to the way groups are already functioning within the church to complete various types of tasks. This discussion can invite deeper reflection on our basic structure for ministry as we begin to see how the pieces of our identity and relationship fit with the ways we prefer to do the work for which we are equipped and called.

Fourth: Recall the definition of *team* as described earlier—"a small number of people with complementary skills who are committed to a common purpose, performance goals, and approach for which they hold themselves mutually accountable" (from *The Wisdom of Teams* by Katzenbach and Smith, page 45), and invite comparison and discussion.

<u>Task Type Preference</u>	<u>May Be Frustrated by</u>	<u>Probably Enjoy</u>
A. Project	Committees	Focused, Short-Term Ministry
B. Work	Boards, Councils, Committees	Hands-On Missions
C. Process	Hands-On Missions	Boards, Councils, Committees
D. Fellowship	Boards, Councils, Committees	Social Ministry, Circles

Fifth: Collect the surveys and record the results on the Group Profile Grid. Also, confirm the totals for each type and record them on the PCL Summary Sheet, noting patterns and anomalies.

Spirituality Web	Individual	Corporate
Head	7	27
Heart	24	18
Pilgrim	10	3
Mystic	5	2
Servant	6	6
Crusader	1	0
Task Types		
Project	19	
Work	9	
Process	3	
Fellowship	12	

Group Profile Grid

Spiritual Gifts Cluster	Leadership/ Interaction Style	Spirituality Type Individual	Spirituality Type Corporate	Task Type
Organizing	Pleaser	Pilgrim	Head	Fellowship
Organizing	Director	Head	Head	Project
Witnessing	Thinker	Servant	Heart	Process

TASK TYPE DESCRIPTIONS

(*Examples of each type appear in italics.*)

A. Project

People who prefer the Project type of task like to see programs, ministries, or events through from start to finish—planning, organizing, implementing, and evaluating all aspects of a project.

Five young adults are asked to create an alternative worship experience for college students. They are to develop the style of worship and the format, set the time and location, recruit musicians, liturgists, and speakers, and create the promotional resources within a six-month time frame.

B. Work

People who prefer the Work type of task like to do hands-on work, without having to bother with the preplanning and organizing. This group wants to be active on the front line.

Men and women volunteer to attend a work camp to build wheelchair-accessible ramps for low-income dwellings. The planning and preparation for the project is done by the Ministry Area on Missions, but the work is done by a one-time team.

C. Process

People who prefer a Process task type enjoy doing the brain-work around the committee table with pen, paper, and planning. This group hands work tasks off to those who prefer them.

Members of a congregation gather to brainstorm ideas for a new church ministry. Members discuss community needs, existing church resources, people's interests and passions, and hopes and dreams for the future. The group prioritizes their ideas and refers their proposal to the church council.

D. Fellowship

The people who prefer the Fellowship task type perform tasks together with a sense of community and common purpose. The work done is secondary to the sense of connection and shared experience.

A group of parents of young children develop a play group that they then open to the general public. The group meets socially in the homes of one another to do their planning and preparation. They stay together in the work because they enjoy each other as friends.

TASK TYPE PREFERENCES: INTERPRETIVE HELPS

- Nurturing congregations tend to prefer Fellowship tasks. Outreaching congregations lean toward Work tasks. Witnessing congregations prefer Project tasks. Organizing churches lean toward Project and Process tasks.
- People who prefer Work and Project tasks perform most effectively in closed-ended situations where the specific task, time limits, assignments, and accountability structures are clearly understood. Task forces and short-term ministries will appeal to Project and Work types.
- Process and Fellowship tasks are open-ended, rarely having clearly set boundaries such as a time frame or a focus on a single task. Committees are preferred by Process and Fellowship types.
- People who prefer Work tasks are the most underutilized resource in many of our churches. These people tend to score higher with the Servant spirituality, and they have little or no patience at a committee table. They want to do.
- How can we find ways to broaden the definition of leadership to affirm and maximize the contributions of people who prefer task types that are not in the majority?
- How do we free people to work in the environments that they enjoy most?
- What are the implications of matching gifts, styles, types, and preferences with ministry and mission?
- Who has responsibility for matching people with the work that will energize and fulfill them?

ADDITIONAL INFORMATION

Five Leadership Groups (Primary Responsibilities)

Board: oversight of the church, holding it to its mission, articulating its vision

Council: long-range, strategic planning, visioning

Committee: organizing ongoing work of the church, implementing strategic plan

Task Force: planning, designing, implementing, and evaluating specific tasks/work

Team: performing specific assigned tasks as a small group

Shared Leadership

Leadership no longer refers to an individual; leadership refers to the collective gifts and abilities that leaders bring together in order to fulfill the mission of the organization. Leadership happens in teams.

NOTES

1. Reprinted by permission of Harvard Business School Press. From *The Wisdom of Teams* by Jon R. Katzenbach and Douglas K. Smith. Boston, MA 1993, p. 45. Copyright © 1993 by McKinsey & Company, Inc. All rights reserved.

91

Intermission: A Trip to Dawson

The Dawson United Methodist Church (a fictional name representing a variety of real congregations) enjoys more life and vitality today than it has known at any other time throughout its two-hundred-year history. In a congregation of one hundred sixty members, over one hundred are engaged in some form of ministry or service through the church. Dozens more report that they are ministering to others at their workplaces or homes in new, important ways. Attendance at three different worship services (headed by three separate worship teams) has doubled in just over three years. The leadership of the church is constantly active, but there are few formal meetings. The financial picture for the church is the strongest in years. The Dawson United Methodist Church is a well-known, well-respected presence in the community—emerging in the consciousness of the small town after years of virtual obscurity. While membership has changed little in recent times, the number of people served by the ministries of the church has increased from dozens to hundreds. All of these changes are happening in a community where there has been no net population growth and the economic conditions have worsened.

What accounts for the vitality of the Dawson United Methodist Church? What steps were taken to move the church from decline and a struggle to survive to a position of strength and growth? What lessons can be learned from their experience to help other churches ready to embrace radical change for the renewal and revitalization of their congregations?

In 1994, the Dawson United Methodist Church decided it was time for a change. People in leadership were working hard and faithfully, but the results didn't warrant the effort. Membership was declining, attendance was low, money was tight, and people were complaining of feeling tired and even burned out. The pastor, Karen, felt that her leadership was insufficient to help turn the small church around. Karen believed that the church held great potential for effective ministry, but working harder at the existing system yielded no noticeable improvement. Frustrated, Karen looked outside her local congregation for some help to address the inertia affecting her church. Karen discovered a process called the Profile of Congregational Leadership (PCL).

I (Dan Dick) was called in to lead the PCL process with the Dawson United Methodist Church. Pastor Karen spent weeks in preparation calling church leaders and obtaining their commitment to attend a weekend-long workshop. Her investment of time in approaching members individually yielded impressive results. At the 1993 charge conference, thirty-seven church members had been elected to serve official leadership positions. Karen brought together twenty-eight (76 percent) of the leaders with six other new members to work on the congregation's leadership profile.

We began on Friday evening with an introduction to the process, some conversation about our hopes for the weekend, and a discussion of what it means to discover and do the will of God. Then we moved through the Spiritual Gifts Inventory. We closed the evening by noting the results of our surveys and looking at brief definitions of the various gifts.

In preparation for the Saturday morning session, I gathered the surveys and compiled a composite picture of the primary and secondary gifts of the gathered leadership. Of the thirty-five people surveyed, thirty shared as either primary or secondary gifts Faith, Knowledge, Teaching, or Shepherding. Absent as primary gifts were Evangelism, Compassion, Prophecy, and Leadership. Absent altogether were the gifts of Apostleship, Tongues, Interpretation of Tongues, and Servanthood. Administration, Giving, Exhortation, Discernment, and Wisdom appeared as strong supporting gifts. The commonly acknowledged strength of the Dawson church was education for children and adults. The gifts profile of the congregational sample explained why.

Pastor Karen and the leadership of the Dawson United Methodist Church had labored under the burden that they should be more active in evangelism, outreach, and missions. New committees had been formed to address the ministry needs in these areas, yet nothing seemed to improve. People wrestled with ways to engage in these ministries, but there was no passion or energy for any of the new ideas. In discussing these issues the next morning, we talked about the frustration of trying to do ministry we are not gifted for. An important shift in thinking occurred at the Dawson church as the leadership focused on their gifts for ministry. Instead of compensating for their weaknesses, the people at Dawson chose to build upon their strengths.

We turned our attention to the Leadership/Interaction Styles of the workshop participants. Of the thirty-five people present, twenty-two were Pleasers, seven were Directors, four were Thinkers, and two were Dreamers. This mix was not unusual. In almost every church setting, like-styled people usually gravitate toward each other. One style comes to dominate all others. Since effective leadership depends on a clear balance of styles and the ability of different styles to work well together, it was important for the Dawson church to examine the implications of having a Pleaser-heavy leadership base. Pleasers are people-oriented. They work hard to build strong relationships and resolve conflict. However, Pleasers are not highly creative or innovative. They do not step forward to take charge. They can be slow at making decisions, and often they are sidetracked by issues of lesser importance. Pleasers are very good at maintaining what already exists, but they rarely venture into new territory. This assessment was remarkably true of the Dawson United Methodist Church.

Following lunch, we turned our attention to the Spirituality Types of the individuals and the congregational experience at Dawson. As individuals, there was a strong balance between Head and Heart spiritualities—sixteen Head and thirteen Heart. There were four Mystics, four Servants, and one Pilgrim, but no Crusaders. Three of the participants had ties between their predominant types and felt each weighed equally, so we allowed the ties to stay in the results. When we reflected on the corporate Spirituality Type of the Dawson United Methodist Church, thirty-one agreed that the church had a pre-dominant Head approach. Four said that the predominant type was Heart. No one felt that Dawson had a dominant Mystic, Pilgrim, Crusader, or Servant type. The clustering of gifts, interaction styles, and Spirituality Types explained well why education was such a strength, while missions and outreach were so difficult for the Dawson church.

We completed the process with the Task Type Preference Survey. The majority of participants preferred working together for the sense of fellowship. Sixteen people listed fellowship first, thirteen selected project, five chose work, and one preferred process.

During the summary discussions, it became clear that the Dawson United Methodist Church could build upon its strengths of relationship building, fellowship, knowledge and teaching, Head and Heart spiritual experiences, and some solid organizational skills. It was also agreed that a good deal of time and energy were being wasted on programs, ministries, and practices that the congregation was not gifted to accomplish.

Prior to the Profile of Congregational Leadership, the Dawson United Methodist Church was primarily a once-a-week, Sunday morning enterprise. Emphasis was given to a variety of Sunday school classes for both children and adults. Attendance at Sunday morning worship averaged seventy to seventy-five at the single traditional service, and around fifty in Sunday school. Most of the non-Sunday activities consisted of commit-tee meetings, work days, and occasional suppers, craft bazaars, and bake sales. Following the PCL, the defining question was, "What would the Dawson United Methodist Church look like as a seven-day-a-week learning/teaching church?"

Over a three-year period, Dawson United Methodist Church built upon its gifts for Education and Shepherding by increasing the number of learning opportunities. Daw-son became the home of adult and children's literacy programs and adult continuing education programs in the evenings. Located in a commuter area where young parents needed to leave for work one or two hours before daycare facilities opened, Dawson became a drop-off center where preschoolers could receive a good breakfast and learn Bible stories and songs. Dawson also opened its doors in the afternoons so that latchkey kids could come to the church to have a snack and do their homework. Adults were on hand to tutor and provide supervision.

After long conversations, the leadership of the church decided it would be better to offer two different types of worship instead of blending the needs of Head and Heart into one service. Gifted individuals within the two Spirituality Types worked together to develop the unique services. In the middle of the second year, a third group formed to create a contemplative, Mystic-oriented service. Pastor Karen worked with a small group of church leaders to share in the preaching and worship leading.

During the three years following the PCL, worship attendance rose to almost two hundred each week, while over one hundred fifty children and adults take part in some form of Christian education each week. The church has been able to almost triple its budget, which is fully subscribed by annual giving. Dawson United Methodist Church holds only one fundraiser each year now, with 100 percent of the proceeds going to missions. Dawson struggled for years to improve their ministries of outreach, missions, and evangelism. Only by focusing on their gifts for education were the leaders of the Dawson United Methodist Church able to realize this desire.

Reflecting on the Dawson experience late in 1999, Ken, the lay leader of the congregation, remarked, "It's too bad we had such great increases in our numbers because it masks the real value of the whole experience. Even if we had never gained a member or received another dollar, it would have been worth it. Before that weekend we were all tired and cranky, really burned-out. People were giving four or five hours a week to the church and complaining that it was way too much. After we expanded our program there were some people spending twenty hours at the church and loving every minute of it. When we were trying to be something we weren't, everyone was exhausted, but when we began living out of our gifts it was like we had energy to burn. You have never seen such passion!"

The Dawson experience is a common experience—churches thrive when they live from their gifts. One definition of faithful stewardship is to manage wisely and well what we have been given by God. Unfortunately, too often we waste time trying to manage what we don't have instead of managing what we do have. Dawson discovered who they were, who God gifted and called them to be, and a way to feel good about themselves.

CHAPTER 6

Beyond Information
to Transformation

The church of the new millennium will be open to new ways of being, responsive to the needs of the individuals who are the church—gifted, graced, hungry to serve, and eager to connect with God and one another in meaningful ways. Out of this new approach, shared call and vision will continually emerge and evolve, leading to the development of systems and structures best suited to the people who are the church in the world. It is not the work of the people to build up the church, it is the work of the church to build up the people as church, to equip them for ministry and mission.

Spiritual gifts-based ministry, rare in The United Methodist Church, focuses on the people—their gifts and passions and their sense of call and Christian vocation. It strives to develop spiritual gifts into highly responsive conduits for skilled and talented servants and to deploy gifted Christians in ministry within the congregation and beyond to the community and world. There is commitment to inclusiveness, to expanding the circle of leadership, to valuing the gifts of all people—the gifts of those on the fringes or new to the community as well as the dominant gifts of established leaders at the center.

Spiritual gifts discovery is not an end in itself. The PCL yields no statistically reliable information. All of the tools are self-report surveys and highly subjective. So what do we do with what we've learned? How do we become a gifts-based church? How do we make the crucial move from program to process?

STAGES OF THE FAITH JOURNEY

Spiritual growth as a process can be seen clearly through the lens of the stages of human growth. Just as people move from conception through birth, early childhood and adolescence, to adulthood and full maturity, so individuals and faith communities begin at spiritual conception and grow through the various stages to maturity, the full stature of the body of Christ (Ephesians 4:13). At full maturity, the body of Christ is able to honor the needs and abilities of individuals wherever they are in their journey of faith. And whatever our spiritual gifts are, individually and collectively, they will provide a uniquely suitable opening for the power of the Holy Spirit to reach out through our hearts and carry on the work of transformation from discipleship through true fellowship to faithful stewardship.

It is essential to remember that this progression is more cyclical than linear and that one of the most critical elements of maturity is humility. Growth is not an excuse to boast of our position but a new opportunity each moment to deepen our knowledge of the world and experience of the living God.

We begin at conception, with those not yet born into the Christian faith. Some are seeking connection with a life of faith for the very first time or reigniting a spark that time and circumstance have all but extinguished. Others have explored alternative spiritualities and are still restless. Certainly, some have actively turned their backs to faith. When in this stage, our focus is entirely on our current reality, and we need to be met where we are. If we are going to say yes to any possibility of relationship with God, tender care and patience are required. It is essential to have our stories heard, to be accepted as we are.

Stages of the Journey of Faith

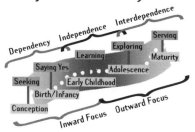

The birthing and infancy of the life of faith is a stage of deep dependence on the guidance and patience of others. Throughout this stage, we believe that the world revolves around us, and our primary motivation is comfort. This is a time for learning the stories of faith and absorbing the ideas and attitudes of the faith community. When we come to the table to be fed, milk is our proper food (1 Corinthians 3:2).

Next comes early childhood, when our first attempts at independence look more like tantrums than thoughtful exercise. The relationship with God is still self-centered, and people ask, "What can a life of faith do for me?" This is a time of pushing back against doctrine and structure, testing boundaries and steadfastness. A faith community that is not clear in its focus or beliefs will not stand up to this test.

During the adolescent phase of the maturing life of faith, the inward focus of comfort, learning, and dependence will begin to shift outward. Deeper exploration and understanding of God's call in and on our lives awakens us to the needs of others. Experiments in independence are more purposeful here, developing through a sense of mission and call. We seek opportunities to try on some of our growing understanding, to spread our wings a bit. If one system for ministry is too rigid, we will simply seek elsewhere.

As we turn our focus outward, moving toward adulthood, we receive more freedom and trust to follow God's leading with integrity. This is a time of independence and great personal growth. It is also a time when we begin to see the real value of community in our journey of faith. As we become increasingly aware that the Spirit burns within us, we are able to see Christ in one another. We begin to understand what real love is, and what it might cost.

True maturity as a community of faith, however, requires that we recognize another stage in the journey. At this interdependent stage—this maturity in the Christian life—individuals who are filled with purpose and provided with the means to live out their call will inevitably feel the need to reconnect in community for both renewal and service. We want to share what we have learned with others, and we need to be fully seen in new ways. It is at this point that many churches fail, and gifted, dedicated leaders burn out or become bored and drift away. The common table of spiritual growth needs to offer meat for the mature Christian as well as milk for the infant.

The journey of faith plus spiritual gifts explored and developed through the means of grace equals the ability to fulfill our mission as the body of Christ. In The United Methodist Church, we have a picture of what a mature church process looks like. The Primary Task, outlined in Chapter 1 (pages 20-21), shows a cycle of ministry lived out completely in all aspects of our ministry: reaching out and receiving, relating to God, nurturing and strengthening people in the faith, and sending them out to live transformed and transforming lives. The Primary Task is a synergistic process. The journey doesn't end when people are equipped and sent. They need to be received where they are, related to God in new ways, further nurtured and strengthened to continuously open the avenues of grace.

DEVELOPMENT: THE MEANS OF GRACE

They devoted themselves to the apostles' teaching and fellowship, to the breaking of bread and the prayers.

—Acts 2:42

This verse describes how the first church that formed after Pentecost chose to develop their gifts. Their numbers grew and they performed great miracles and wonders in the community. These were also the activities of Jesus and the disciples—study, prayer, fellowship, communion, and service. These are the means of grace, the ways in which we can provide a wider avenue for God's grace to work within and through us. While each of us is uniquely gifted by God, it is up to us to learn about these gifts and to develop our abilities to use them faithfully. By engaging in the means of grace, we can continuously focus on our gifts, deepen our understanding of our gifts, and work to improve the way we use them. The means of grace offer nourishment, instruction, encouragement, challenge—access to all the provisions we will need for the journey of faith. And, as our work with the Spirituality Web reveals, we all experience the means of grace in different ways.

Prayer

God is the author of all our gifts and is the source of true understanding about how the gifts are best used. In taking time to pray to God, we allow God to direct our service and open us to the endless possibilities for Christian service. It is not the intention of our prayers to ask God to show us how to use our gifts, but our intention is to ask that God reveal all the many ways we live out of our gifts each and every day. As we see our gifts revealed, then we seek God's guidance in ways to develop and improve them. We enter into a partnership with God to be wise stewards of the valuable gifts of the Spirit.

Scripture

The Bible is full of stories of gifted people interacting and living in the light of God. Both Old and New Testaments offer fine illustrations of teachers, healers, apostles, servants, evangelists, and men and women with all the other gifts used to transform the world and serve the needs of others. The church itself is built upon the rich and diverse gifts of the people. In reading the Scriptures with an eye toward the spiritual gifts employed by the people and reflecting upon the meaning of those gifts for our own lives, we begin to see the power and the possibilities that our gifts provide to us.

As people grow in their faith, they need constant exposure to the study of Scripture, to the theological reflections of great thinkers through time, and to the devotional and spiritual writings of the mothers and fathers of our Christian heritage. Many congregations embrace the concept that we cannot be in meaningful ministry to others without being intentional in our own study and reflection.

Lord's Supper

John Wesley did not name worship among the means of grace. Wesley offered a much broader definition of worship than what we generally encounter today. Wherever any of the means of grace are faithfully practiced, there you will find authentic Christian worship. Wesley specifically named the celebration of the Lord's Supper as a means of grace. The Lord's Supper is a clear example of what God does for us through the body, blood, and spirit of Jesus Christ. In Communion, we are made "one with Christ, one with each other, and one in ministry to all the world."[1] At the very center of our understanding of spiritual gifts is the image of the body of Christ. When we participate in the sacrament of Holy Communion, we step forward to accept our place in Christ's body as well as affirm our commitment to our community in Christ.

Fasting/Abstinence

No Christian discipline has fallen further from popular practice than fasting. Originally, fasting served both the spiritual purpose of honoring God for God's bounty and providence and the practical purpose of making the limited resources of a community spread across the course of the entire year. In our culture, where few of our church members face imminent starvation, the practical motivation is lacking, and the sense that God is our provider—as opposed to the idea that we earn our own way, and no one gives us anything—is virtually nonexistent.

The practice of fasting in spiritual community is an open invitation. When we commit to fast together, we are making a sacrifice that yields solidarity. When we agree together to endure our discomfort in prayer and mutual support, we build community. When we feel hunger and the subsequent pangs and pains, we are reminded that self-sufficiency is an illusion, and that true strength comes through relationship with God and neighbor.

Another approach to fasting in our day is to determine appropriate sacrifices that enable us to focus on God, community, and world. Some people give up watching television for a month to devote time to prayer, study, or community service. Some folks turn off the phone for a few hours each day to read, reflect, or create intentional family or relationship time. Some give up talking for a day and spend the silence listening for the voice of God or the cry of the needy. There is no right way to abstain, but there is wondrous power in doing without something that we often take for granted.

Small-Group Sharing (Christian Conference)

John Wesley encouraged Christian believers to engage in regular conversation about their faith journeys (Christian conference). In small-group class meetings, Christians prayed together, studied together, planned acts of mercy and service, sang songs, and asked questions of one another such as "How is it with your soul?" Similar groups today provide ideal settings in which to explore our spiritual gifts and to discover together the will of God for our lives.

Conversation centered upon the gifts of the Spirit helps to keep the gifts in focus and allows us to share the way we understand our giftedness. When we talk about our gifts—the ways we have used them in the past, the ways in which we live from them day to day, and the hopes we have for developing our gifts in the future—they become a central part of our lives, and they give shape to our journey of faith. The benefit of sharing in a small group is that we enter into a covenant relationship of accountability, holding us to a path of continual development and faithful stewardship.

Participants in the PCL process have reported success with Affinity/Fellowship groups. These groups help to explore a variety of dimensions of spiritual giftedness. Here are some examples:

- Form three groups: those gifted with Faith, Prophecy, Wisdom, Knowledge, and Discernment; those with Healing, Miracles, and Serving; and those with Teaching, Leadership, Administration, Giving, and Helping. Ask each group to create a description of what they believe the primary work of the congregation is, complete with what kinds of resourcing that requires. Bring the groups together to compare/contrast results. (Of course, you can mix-and-match gifts in a variety of ways—reflecting the sample of gifts in your congregation.)

- Allow members with the same primary gift to discuss in small groups what they believe their gifts mean for ministry within the church, being as specific as possible. Then report the discussions together as a large group.
- Form groups of six, where no primary gift is represented more than once in any group, and discuss ways that the team might combine their gifts for an effective ministry or service. This exercise challenges the group to see the connectedness of spiritual gifts and how gifts might complement each other in new ways.
- Congregational Sharing: As a large group, list all the primary gifts on one sheet of newsprint and all the current working groups (committees, teams, boards, task forces, and so forth) on another. Analyze which tasks well utilize, moderately utilize, or underutilize the giftedness of the leadership team. Which tasks require gifts not manifest within the leadership sample?

Acts of Mercy and Service

Doing, not just knowing, is the essential ingredient to living out of our gifts. To know our gifts is important, but until we actively employ our gifts, we are hiding our light under a bushel. We will not be comfortable using our gifts without regular and intentional practice. We can start small and work our way up, but still we need to start. We can plan ways to use our gifts as well as identify places where our gifts are already employed. Talking with others can be an excellent way to gain perspective on the gifts that we actively share.

Many churches have developed Act/Reflect opportunities. Act/Reflect opportunities are exercises in which a group engages in a service linked closely to their primary gifts. Then members come together to share their reflections and what they learned. One church assembled a group of people with the gifts of Compassion, Exhortation, and Healing and took them to a variety of hospitals and nursing homes each week. Then the group spent one evening together each week to share their thoughts, feelings, and memories from the previous week. Without exception, every member of the group reported that the reflecting portion of the Act/Reflect opportunity was of the greatest value. They also shared that, for the most part, they couldn't remember a time in their church when they were given the opportunity to reflect at all. Generally we act, but rarely do we reflect.

DEPLOYMENT: MATURING LOVE

As our gifts are developed and our understanding of God's will grows, it is essential to deploy our gifts in community. It is in community that we grow as disciples of Jesus Christ and as stewards of the gospel. We are part of a body, the body of Christ. Our gifts are given for the upbuilding of that body. They are intended to promote harmony, to strengthen unity, to help us better love and care for one another and for the hurting world. Try them on. Share what you learn with others. Practice. Pray.

Where and how do we use our gifts? In the chapter following the gifts passage in 1 Corinthians 12, Scripture provides an answer, a "more excellent way." First Corinthians 13:1-13, so familiar in other contexts, speaks to us of the maturing of love, growing toward perfection through loving relationship.

What is the relationship between love and the spiritual gifts? The gifts are one way God expresses God's love for us. As we mature in our ability to respond in love, we will use our gifts in service to one another and the hurting world. This is the more excellent way.

As we consider the various activities and ministries of the church, there are infinite numbers of ways to allow our spiritual gifts, working through our skills and talents, to serve the needs of a vital, growing community of faith. As our gifts are developed and our understanding of God's will grows, we link and deploy our gifts so that others may come to know and be known, to share in the joy and fulfillment of service and witness in the name of Christ.

A critical function of the leadership of a local congregation is to make it not only easy but imperative for people to put their gifts to work. Here are some ways we can use our congregational system to help deploy the gifts for ministry:

- **Set aside an Administrative Council/Council on Ministries/Church Council meeting to ask some "what if" questions:**
  — What if we created ministry teams based on gifts instead of committees?
  — What if we dissolved the formal structures and started from zero?
  — What if our existing committees stopped functioning for the next six months? What would happen to the church? How would we use that time instead? How might we use more of our "leadership" time for spiritual centering and practicing the means of grace?
  — How can we take spiritual gifts discovery to the next level and expand our "data" base?
  — How do we raise awareness of spiritual giftedness and help people to understand that there is need for change in certain structures and practices based on spiritual gifts discovery and development?
- **Use the 3-every-6 process.** Focus on three gifts every six months and ask the following questions:
  — How do these gifts shape the ministry of our church?
  — What new ministries could emerge as we work to develop and improve these gifts?
  — How do these gifts support each other? How are they complementary? How are they supplementary? What other gifts could strengthen them?
  — How might we better honor the use of these gifts through our ministry?

- **Use the Inside/Outside Approach**. As the leadership of a congregation evaluates its plan and program for ministry, our spiritual gifts challenge us to seek ways to use the gifts both within the community of faith as well as out in the world in our ministry in daily life. Here are some helpful reflection questions:
  - How can we use each gift at church, at work, at home, while driving, while talking on the phone, when we shop, when we play, and so forth?
  - What if our committee on lay leadership nominated people for one church-related ministry and one community-focused ministry each year?
  - What if each new program in the church was matched by one new program focused on serving a constituency outside the congregation?
  - How might we help people better understand what it means to live from their gifts seven days a week?
- **Plan a Churchwide festival/celebration/visioning.** Spiritual gifts are a big deal, but they haven't been presented as such for a long, long time. The time has come to make a big deal of our spiritual gifts once more. Celebrations, fairs, recognition dinners, and gifts festivals are a few ways that some churches have adopted to elevate awareness and understanding about the importance of spiritual gifts. One Iowa congregation held a community fair and administered the Spiritual Gifts Inventory to over three hundred non–church members of the community.

CONCLUSION

As you consider the various activities and ministries of the church and the critical needs of our world, there are infinite numbers of ways to allow our spiritual gifts, working through our skills, talents, styles, and Spirituality Types, to serve the needs of a vital, growing community of faith. A gifts-based church begins with the identity of the people and God's call, and it designs the best possible systems for living out that call in community.

As our gifts develop and our understanding of God's will grows, we link and deploy our gifts so that others may come to know and be known, to share in the joy and fulfillment of service and witness in the name of Christ. It is in community that we grow as disciples of Jesus Christ and as stewards of the mysteries of God. This healthy, organic cycle of growth began with the earliest Spirit-led, gifts-based communities and finds its fullest expression in the body of Christ joyfully committed to, and constantly seeking to live out, the will of God.

When we love in response to God's love for us, the whole community benefits. But what happens in us? How do we know we are doing it right?

- when duty starts to feel like passion;
- when the fruits of the Spirit, the fruit that will last—"love, joy, peace, patience, kindness, generosity, faithfulness, gentleness, and self-control" (Galatians 5:22-23)—are more present than absent, even in times of trial;

- when you are feeling more satisfied with the course of your life and closer to fulfillment of your deepest desires;
- when evidence of joy abounds in your congregation;
- when the people you serve and touch in your lives cannot help seeing the light that shines through you—the breath of life, the spark of holy fire that fills and transforms you so that you and they may participate in the transformation of the world.

There is no one right way to develop and discover our gifts. What is important is that we try some things that feel right and see what the Holy Spirit will provide.

NOTES

1. From "Services of Word and Table" and "The Great Thanksgivings," in *The United Methodist Book of Worship.* © 1992 by The United Methodist Publishing House; pages 33-77. Used by permission.

Appendixes

Profile of Congregational Leadership
Process Schedule

Profile of Congregational Leadership—
Interpretive Matrices

Phase of Life Context

Follow-Up Exercises

Spiritual Gifts Data

"The Next Best Thing to Jesus Christ"

Profile of Congregational Leadership Process Schedule

The Profile of Congregational Leadership (PCL) event requires *at least* 9 1/2 hours of contact time (and can therefore offer .9 CEU's—continuing education units—with approval of the Board of Ordained Ministry). This event may be done over a two- or three-day period. It is strongly recommended that you do not attempt the PCL in a single day. Individuals need time not only to process the tools and their responses but also to integrate the information as it is presented. It is vital to give participants time to make sense of the experience as it unfolds. Below are some guidelines to follow in developing the PCL workshop format. Also included is a checklist of processes and tasks to keep in mind as you prepare and proceed.

The materials mentioned in this section as "overheads" or "templates" are intended for use with an overhead projector. These files can be downloaded from the website, printed out, and copied onto transparencies for the projector. They include summary templates for each of the tools. All data for these templates can be taken from the PCL Summary Sheet. These materials are helpful in illustrating and guiding the group process.

1ST DAY—EVENING

Leader Notes: Arrive early to check room set-up. (See the checklist on page 116). Make sure needed materials are available, including nametags.

1/2 hour   Begin with singing and devotions.

1 hour   Conduct the Spiritual Gifts Inventory.
If using overheads, the SGI Scoring Guide and SGI Key can be helpful visual aids.

Spiritual Gifts Scoring Guide	Spiritual Gifts Key	
7 – Always	1. Wisdom	11. Compassion
6 – Almost Always	2. Knowledge	12. Healing
5 – Often	3. Administration	13. Discernment
4 – Sometimes	4. Apostleship	14. Teaching
3 – Rarely	5. Shepherding	15. Helping
2 – Almost Never	6. Faith	16. Evangelism
1 – Never	7. Miracles	17. Servanthood
	8. Prophecy	18. Exhortation
	9. Leadership	19. Tongues
	10. Giving	20. Interpretation of Tongues

1 hour   Present definitions of Spiritual Gifts. See the website for overhead descriptions of each of the gifts.
Record gifts on the Personal Profile Puzzles.
Collect Personal Profile Puzzles from participants.
Close the evening session with prayer.

Leader Preparation for the Next Session

✔ Calculate and record the Spiritual Gifts Cluster category on each
participant's Personal Profile Puzzle.

✔ Record the name and primary/secondary spiritual gifts and cluster
category of each participant on the Group Profile Grid.

Profile of Congregational Leadership: Group Profile (					
Last Name	**First Name**	**Primary Spiritual Gift**	**Secondary Spiritual Gifts**	**Spiritual Gifts Cluster**	Le: Int
Anderson	Alan	Giving	Helping, Administration, Knowledge	Organizing	
Blass	Beth	Leadership	Healing, Teaching, Faith	Organizing	
Crane	Carol	Faith	Healing, Prophecy, Compassion	Witnessing	

✔ Tabulate and record total numbers of primary/secondary spiritual
gifts on the PCL Summary Sheet.

✔ Calculate and record the Spiritual Gifts Cluster for the group on
the PCL Summary Sheet.

Profile of Congregational Leadership Summary Sheet *Putting the Pieces Together*		
Spiritual Gifts	Primary	Secondary
Administration	3	12
Apostleship	0	1
Compassion	2	7
Discernment	0	6
Evangelism	0	5
Exhortation	0	4
Faith	13	22
Giving	3	7
Healing	11	19
Helping	4	10
Interpretation of Tongues	0	2
Knowledge	2	12
Leadership	1	7
Miracles	3	15
Prophecy	1	10
Servanthood	1	14
Shepherding	0	1
Teaching	6	8
Tongues	0	0
Wisdom	0	5
Spiritual Gifts Cluster		
Nurturing —152	130	22
Outreaching —158	110	48
Witnessing —341	300	41
Organizing —60	60	0
Leadership/Interaction Styles		
Director		

✔ If using overheads, record totals of primary/secondary spiritual gifts, in descending order, on the Spiritual Gifts Concentration templates.

Spiritual Gifts Concentration

	Primary	Secondary

✔ If using overheads, record total number of participants in each Spiritual Gifts Cluster on the Spiritual Gifts Clusters template.

Spiritual Gifts Clusters

Nurturing	Outreaching
P-__ __ S-__ __	P-__ __ S-__ __
Witnessing	**Organizing**
P-__ __ S-__ __	P-__ __ S-__ __

2ND DAY—MORNING

1/2 hour Begin with singing and devotions.

1/2 hour Return Personal Profile Puzzles.

Present results of Spiritual Gifts Inventory.

Define Spiritual Gifts Clusters and present Spiritual Gifts cluster results, using the Spiritual Gifts Clusters overhead template if desired.

1/2 hour Hear responses, questions, insights, and so forth.

Break

1 hour Conduct the Leadership/Interaction Styles Survey (including small-group discussion, Stress Paths, and Harmonizing). See the website for presentation overheads on Leadership/Interaction Styles.

1/2 hour Hear responses, questions, insights—include some discussion of relationship between Spiritual Gifts and Leadership/Interaction Styles.

Collect Personal Profile Puzzles.

Leader Preparation for the Next Session

✔ Record the Leadership/Interaction Style(s) of each participant on the Group Profile Grid.

ational Leadership: Group Profile Grid				
imary tual Gift	Secondary Spiritual Gifts	Spiritual Gifts Cluster	Leadership/ Interaction Style	Sp In
iving	Helping, Administration, Knowledge	Organizing	Pleaser	
lership	Healing, Teaching, Faith	Organizing	Director	
aith	Healing, Prophecy, Compassion	Witnessing	Thinker	

✔ Tabulate and record total numbers of Leadership/Interaction Styles on the PCL Summary Sheet.

Shepherding	0	1
Teaching	6	8
Tongues	0	0
Wisdom	0	5
Spiritual Gifts Cluster		
Nurturing —152	130	22
Outreaching —158	110	48
Witnessing —341	300	41
Organizing —60	60	0
Leadership/Interaction Styles		
Director	14	
Dreamer	7	
Pleaser	17	
Thinker	8	
Spirituality Web	Individual	Corporate
Head		
Heart		
Pilgrim		

✔ If using overheads, calculate percentages and record these with totals of Leadership/Interaction Styles on the Leadership/Interaction Styles Summary template.

Leadership/Interaction Styles	
Thinker ―― (――%) (7% church, 18%)	Director ―― (――%) (11% church, 26%)
Pleaser ―― (――%) (43% church, 32% pop)	Dreamer ―― (――%) (39% church, 24% pop)

2ND DAY—AFTERNOON

1/2 hour   Begin with singing and devotions.

1/4 hour   Return Personal Profile Puzzles.

Present results of Leadership/Interaction Styles.

1 hour   Conduct Spirituality Web (Individual and Corporate). See the website for presentation overheads on the Spirituality Web.

1/4 hour   Hear responses, questions, insights, and so forth.

Include dialogue on integration of Spiritual Gifts, Leadership/Interaction Styles, and Spirituality Web.

Collect Personal Profile Puzzles.

Break

Leader Preparation for the Session After the Break

✔ Record the Individual and Corporate Spirituality Type(s) of each participant on the Group Profile Grid.

roup Profile Grid				
Spiritual ifts Cluster	Leadership/ Interaction Style	Spirituality Type Individual	Spirituality Type Corporate	Tas
Organizing	Pleaser	Pilgrim	Head	
Organizing	Director	Head	Head	
Witnessing	Thinker	Servant	Heart	

✔ Tabulate and record total numbers of Individual and Corporate Spirituality Types on the PCL Summary Sheet.

Witnessing	—341	300	41
Organizing	—60	60	0
Leadership/Interaction Styles			
Director		14	
Dreamer		7	
Pleaser		17	
Thinker		8	
Spirituality Web		Individual	Corporate
Head		7	27
Heart		24	18
Pilgrim		10	3
Mystic		5	2
Servant		6	6
Crusader		1	0
Task Types			
Project			
Work			
Process			
Fellowship			

✔ If using overheads, record totals of Individual and Corporate
   Spirituality Types on the Spirituality Web Summary templates.

Spirituality Web Summary

Crusader Head		Crusader Head
Servant Heart		Servant Heart
Individual		**Corporate**
Mystic Pilgrim		Mystic Pilgrim

✔ If using overheads, record results of Spirituality Web and
   Leadership/Interaction Styles on the Web/LIS Cross-Reference
   Matrix template.

Spirituality Web/L.I.S. Cross Reference						
Web ??? L.I.S.S.	Head	Heart	Pilgrim	Mystic	Servant	Crusader
Director						
Dreamer						
Pleaser						
Thinker						

2ND DAY—AFTER THE BREAK

1/2 hour   Return Personal Profile Puzzles.

Conduct Task Type Preferences Survey. See the website for a
presentation overhead on Task Type Preferences.

By show of hands, tabulate totals of Task Types and, if using
overheads, record these totals on the Task Type Summary template.

Task Type Preferences

A. Project ____
B. Work ____
C. Process ____
D. Fellowship ____

October 2000 Equipped for Every Good Work. Dan R. Dick & Barbara Miller

1/2 hour   Hear responses, questions, insights, and so forth.
Include dialogue on integration of information from all four tools.
Collect Personal Profile Puzzles.

1 hour   Discuss next steps: follow-up gatherings, development, and deployment. Be sure to lift up resources and ideas for deeper exploration. The group will be hungry for guidance and completely overwhelmed by this time. Think grace. Distribute evaluation form. Use the "I Hate Evaluations" sheet, available from the website, or use one of your own choosing.

Leader Preparation (while participants fill out evaluation)

✔ Record the Task Type(s) of each participant on the Group Profile Grid.

rofile Grid				
al ster	Leadership/ Interaction Style	Spirituality Type Individual	Spirituality Type Corporate	Task Type
ng	Pleaser	Pilgrim	Head	Fellowship
ng	Director	Head	Head	Project
ng	Thinker	Servant	Heart	Process

✔ Tabulate and record total numbers of Task Types on the PCL Summary Sheet.

Leadership	1	7
Miracles	3	15
Prophecy	1	10
Servanthood	1	14
Shepherding	0	1
Teaching	6	8
Tongues	0	0
Wisdom	0	5
Spiritual Gifts Cluster		
Nurturing —152	130	22
Outreaching —158	110	48
Witnessing —341	300	41
Organizing —60	60	0
Leadership/Interaction Styles		
Director	14	
Dreamer	7	
Pleaser	17	
Thinker	8	
Spirituality Web	Individual	Corporate
Head	7	27
Heart	24	18
Pilgrim	10	3
Mystic	5	2
Servant	6	6
Crusader	1	0
Task Types		
Project	19	
Work	9	
Process	3	
Fellowship	12	

Collect Evaluations.

Return Personal Profile Puzzles.

Close with Prayer/Sending Forth.

GROUP LEADER CHECKLIST

3 Weeks Prior to the Workshop

_____ Arrange to have one copy of every handout made for each participant.

_____ If using overheads and summary templates, download, print, and copy onto transparencies for use with projector.

_____ Make arrangements for room set-up (people need to be around tables), refreshments, speaker's table or podium, overhead projector, screen, pencils, and nametags. It is also a good idea to arrange for newsprint, easel, markers, and masking tape. Check on housing (if you travel a distance), meal arrangements (how will all the people be fed?), availability of Bibles, hymnals, piano (pianist?) or CD/tape player, and so forth.

1 Week Prior to the Event

_____ Double-check earlier arrangements. (No, seriously do this!)

_____ Make sure you have transparencies, any handouts needed, copies of resources you want to lift up, music you may use, devotions.

_____ Go through all the materials as a refresher—the less you are tied to notes, the less tension people feel going through a very intense experience.

Follow-Up

_____ **Within 2 Weeks of the Event:** Process all the information. Look for "red" (warning), "green" (celebration), and "blue" (interesting, unique) flags, and begin raising questions. Don't wait too long; do it while the event is still fresh in your mind.

_____ **Within 4-6 Weeks of the Event:** Compile all group profile data along with your observations and questions into report format.

_____ Distribute the finished profile to designated follow-up group.

_____ **3 Months After the Event:** Examine process status.

_____ **6 Months After the Event:** Examine process status.

Profile of Congregational Leadership—Interpretive Matrices

One of the greatest benefits of the Profile of Congregational Leadership (PCL) is to the individual. Christian disciples are constantly seeking ways to better understand who they are and who God is calling them to be. Sometimes the results of the PCL survey tools are not clear to the people who respond to them. The Interpretive Matrices lay out a cross-reference of Spirituality Type and Leadership Interaction Style under each Spiritual Gift. When someone asks, "But what does it mean to be a Head-Director-Evangelist?" these matrices offer a "jumping-off" place from which to explore.

These matrices are simply interpretive tools to help you familiarize yourself with the possible combinations of gifts, types, and styles. They are not scientifically drafted or statistically supported. They are anecdotal findings, but they can be useful in discussing how gifts, interaction styles, and Spirituality Types work together in the life of the Christian disciple. It is important to use these thumbnail descriptions not to define individuals but merely to provide a starting place for understanding how people with the same gift can live out of that giftedness in significantly different ways.

A brief survey of the matrices will reinforce what a rich and varied tapestry is created when uniquely gifted people with different styles of interaction, both with others and with God, are woven together to form the church. In diversity is strength, creativity, and beauty. These matrices may assist us in helping church members not only to discover and affirm their own place in the body of Christ but also to acknowledge and celebrate the different gifts and graces of others.

ADMINISTRATION

	Head	Heart	Pilgrim
Director	Highly organized; efficient; likes lots of paper; sends memos, letters; good on the phone; task-oriented, likes working alone	Highly organized; likes working with people; good at delegation; organizes people around tasks; good communicator	Effective at preparing opportunities for people to explore important questions of faith and creating safe environments for sharing
Dreamer	Good at long-range planning, development, and organization of new programs	Good at visioning and brainstorming; good at group process and people-based ministries	Proficient at creating brainstorming sessions to explore the "what-if" questions of the Christian faith
Pleaser	Letter writer—sends cards, e-mail, and so forth to keep in touch and keep people notified about important information; takes great minutes	Good at inviting people to participate in programs and events; good at designing fellowship events	Good at organizing fellowship events for people who are new to or unfamiliar with the Christian church
Thinker	Enjoys role of record keeper, bookkeeper, church historian, or similar position involving working alone with paper and pen or computer	Works with a small team of people to make sure that things are organized and set up; may work with one other person (secretary)	Behind-the-scenes worker to create resources to help people explore questions of their faith
	Mystic	**Servant**	**Crusader**
Director	Disciplined and faithful to perform tasks; works better alone than with others; dependable	Good at organizing people and resources to accomplish a task; focused on getting the job done; organizes as a means to an end	Believes that good organization is the key to successful accomplishment of life goal; productivity equals righteousness
Dreamer	Organizes people around the development of spiritual community and faith formation	Good at developing new ministry proposals and initiating processes without developing strategic plan	Able to organize large, audacious programs and ministries
Pleaser	Good at designing retreat and small-group models for spiritual reflection; will create extensive materials for study and reflection	Good at setting up mission projects and community service projects; good at getting a group together to work	Committed to keeping everyone who works together on a project happy
Thinker	Usually develops personal resources for discipline; writes them down and shares them with others	Works to design mission and service projects that others will conduct	Develops the structures, resources, and tools necessary to accomplish important tasks

APOSTLESHIP			
	Head	**Heart**	**Pilgrim**
Director	Designs new ministry plans for taking the gospel to foreign countries or into other cultural settings	Is active in implementing new ministry plans, working on-site to direct the work of missionary/apostles	Moves into a variety of cultural settings to compare important spiritual questions of other faiths with Christianity
Dreamer	Visionary view of spreading the gospel to every nation, to every culture; good at persuading others to get involved	Same as Head/Dreamer but without concern for viability of plan—vision is compelling, doesn't want to clutter the image with details	Holds a visionary view of a grand ecumenism, reconciling the best elements of a variety of traditions with Christianity
Pleaser	Will support the design and development of a missionary outreach to share the gospel; may frequently participate in mission trips/events	Much more likely to participate in missional outreach, and will seek ways to be involved with faith sharing with other cultures at home	Engages in conversation and discussion with others about the need to spread Christian love in other cultures
Thinker	Works behind the scenes to organize, plan, and resource mission/outreach efforts	Most often gives money and moral support to the mission/outreach work of the community; passively involved	Interested in reading and reflecting on comparative religions and the great spiritual writings of the world
	Mystic	**Servant**	**Crusader**
Director	Works with a small group of people to develop spiritual community in a foreign land or different cultural setting	A "doer" on the front line, going into missionary service at home or abroad; usually following a clearly defined plan	Moves into other cultural spheres with the express intention of proclaiming the Christian gospel
Dreamer	More likely to pray for the gospel to be spread than to move into the world to spread it	Unfocused, but deeply committed to sharing the gospel with all nations; desire may exceed ability	Pursues a vision of a worldwide Christianity resembling the kingdom of God come upon the earth
Pleaser	May offer spiritual guidance and direction to people of another culture nearby; emphasis is on building faith community	Missionary material—ready to go to foreign lands, learn new languages, sleep in sleeping bags, and eat food out of a pouch	Creates exciting and interesting experiences where people can encounter the positive and attractive aspects of the Christian faith
Thinker	More likely to pray for the gospel to be spread than to move into the world to spread it	Good team leader for mission training and planning; involved in the entire process of mission/outreach	Gathers information on ways to spread the gospel message with the greatest possible impact; provides support to front-line apostles

COMPASSION		
	Head	**Heart**	**Pilgrim**
Director	Good board-of-directors material for community ministries, helping the poor, the homeless, the outcasts	Brings caregiving ministries to the church where a coordinated effort is designed to meet needs inside and outside the church	Generally committed to serving the physical and spiritual needs of the poor, ill, or homeless in equal measure
Dreamer	Envisions multiple ways for the community to meet the needs of the less fortunate; sees needs that many others miss	Leads by emotion, often the one most passionate to do something for those in need; wants less talk, more action	Good at rallying support for those in need by questioning the status quo and asking people to consider shifting resources from comfort to caring
Pleaser	Up-front person at the soup kitchens and hospitals who makes sure that everyone is greeted, everyone is served	Pushes for caring/outreaching ministries to be central to the life of the community, both internally and externally	Tends to reach out to individuals who are both in need and of a different background to gain understanding as well as offer assistance
Thinker	Good board-of-directors material for community ministries, helping the poor, the homeless, the outcasts	Able to articulate the needs to be met and the resources required; helps to give practical input to the vision of caregiving	Likely to join with ecumenical groups to create the broadest possible plan for serving the needy
	Mystic	**Servant**	**Crusader**
Director	Organizes prayer vigils, fasts, and awareness-raising processes for the congregation	Organizes soup kitchens, homeless shelters, Head Start programs, and so forth; makes the church a center of caring	Champions a specific group and dedicates all resources to fulfilling central needs
Dreamer	Prays, fasts, and visits in hopes of making a difference in the lives of those in need; often more individual in efforts	Initiates Habitat for Humanity–type programs; big-picture doer	Commits to changing the world from a place of pain and suffering to a society of sharing and caring in whatever way possible (or impossible!)
Pleaser	Strives to sensitize the community of faith to the needs of others through intercessory prayer, study, and so forth	Lives and dwells among the lost, the last, and the least in order to give aid and comfort	Will do whatever possible to bring comfort and joy to others, regardless of personal cost
Thinker	May care deeply about the needs of others, but keeps it both personal and private; devoted to praying for others	Probably involved deeply in some form of service to the needy, service about which absolutely no one knows or would ever guess	Generally will study the root causes of poverty, injustice, abuse, and disease with the expectation of finding radical solutions

DISCERNMENT			
	Head	**Heart**	**Pilgrim**
Director	Confident of own opinion/impression of others; uses discernment as an intellectual rather than intuitive tool	Makes decisions based more on intuition than on evidence; works with trusted people, others are ignored	Seeks the feelings and opinions of others and weighs them against personal feelings; deeply understanding of people with doubts, questions, and anxieties about faith
Dreamer	Acts on intuition and seeks ways to confirm feelings through empirical data; highly persuasive once personally convinced	Has clear impressions of right and wrong; looking to find God's will for self and for the community; trusts gut-level feelings implicitly	Visionary, creative; pays close attention to dreams, hunches, and emotional states when making decisions
Pleaser	Quick to share positive impressions; tends to conceal negatives; tends to analyze feelings closely	Quick to share positive impressions; tends to conceal negatives; doesn't think about feelings, simply acts on them	Puts great trust in groups who share common feelings, hunches, or reactions to specific events
Thinker	Analytical and detailed in his or her impressions; gives reasoned arguments to support intuitive feelings	Has highly-reasoned explanations for why he or she feels one way or another; always questioning the validity of teachings	Generally seeks after documented proof that feelings and intuitions are sound and shared by others
	Mystic	**Servant**	**Crusader**
Director	Prayerfully seeks God's guidance and will; shares impressions freely with others; convinced that God will clarify confusion	Looks for individual direction from God to determine right path of action; not much interested in corporate discernment	Very clearly understands purpose and plan for life at an intuitive level; nothing can dissuade this person from what he or she discerns to be the right course
Dreamer	Truly contemplative; feels assured of the rightness of feelings by prayerfully seeking God's will	Totally committed to acting on belief of God's will for his or her life; quick to act on feelings	Reports having his or her life changed by visions, hearing voices, receiving messages, or revelations
Pleaser	Attends to the things that are perceived as right and good, avoiding the bad or evil; usually doesn't share impressions	Will support those who are discerned as good, avoid or oppose those who are perceived as bad	Highly motivational; inspires energy and support for what he or she intuitively knows is right
Thinker	Contemplative theologian; examines the Scriptures and sacred writings for visceral knowledge of truth	Seeks the true path; perpetually correcting course based on feelings and impressions	Seeks to provide a rational argument to prove feelings are legitimate; sometimes legalistic, but always persuasive

121

EVANGELISM		
	Head	**Heart**	**Pilgrim**
Director	Has detailed plan for evangelism, including a comprehensive training, complete with materials and script for faith sharing	Has full-scale commitment to share the faith on a regular basis, usually telling stories of faith rather than relying on Scripture or theology	Invites people to contemplate the meaning of God and Christ by asking questions and offering options for belief
Dreamer	Tells people what a relationship with Jesus Christ will do for them in their lives; focused on relationship with God	Helps people see what a relationship with Jesus will do for them; less with words than with feelings and stories	Shares the many ways that people approach a relationship with Jesus Christ with an openness to the full spectrum from evangelical to liberal theologies
Pleaser	Desires to talk to people about how important Jesus Christ is personally and to share a reasoned account of why he or she believes	Shares stories about how Jesus has touched his or her life with the hope (and intention) that similar experiences may happen to others	Encourages the sharing of faith experiences where people are aware of the hand of God or the leading of the Spirit
Thinker	Provides a detailed and comprehensive argument for the validity of the gospel; will recommend books to read	Provides a deep and critical evaluation of Christian experience and story in order to communicate the validity of the gospel	May work to develop how-to instructions for talking about faith in open and inviting ways
	Mystic	**Servant**	**Crusader**
Director	Deeply personal and usually interacts one-on-one or in a small-group setting; often centered in praying for others to come to know God	Serves the needs of others in a real and tangible way in the name of Jesus Christ	Leads crusades and stadium events to spread the good news of Jesus Christ to everyone possible
Dreamer	Provides a model of centered spiritual living that communicates the power of Christ to others, no words needed	Sets out to save the world one person at a time; whenever service is rendered, there is no doubt that it is done in the name of Jesus	Spreads the good news through pageantry and performance, making the sharing of the gospel a media event
Pleaser	Will direct efforts of personal spiritual discipline toward providing an example for others through prayer and sharing	Serves the needs of others in a tangible way to provide comfort and hope, sharing the good news with people as they will hear it	Makes the gospel fun and interesting, often using humor, music, art, or drama as the medium of communication
Thinker	Will pray and fast for the salvation of the world	Will preach reasoned and inspiring messages of the truth and power of Jesus Christ; often becomes street-corner minister	Often communicates powerful messages in rational, reasonable language to prove the efficacy of Christian belief

EXHORTATION		
	Head	**Heart**	**Pilgrim**
Director	Communicates carefully constructed messages of hope	Regularly offers messages of hope and encouragement to community or congregation	Encourages exploration of questions of faith in a nonjudgmental, hopeful context
Dreamer	Constructs elaborate visions of hope and inspiration to hold before the community or congregation	Sees and shares the most hopeful visions for the future and looks for the best in all people and all situations	Looks for the messages and teachings of hope and healing in Christian Scriptures and other spiritual writings
Pleaser	Sends cards and letters and makes personal visits and phone calls to extend care and concern for others and to offer hope and support	Makes personal contact as a ministry of caring to provide hope and encouragement to those in need	Strives to support and encourage others as they wrestle with issues of faith and belief
Thinker	Provides a reasoned argument, incorporating facts and figures, to communicate hope for the future	Provides encouragement by telling stories and relating illustrations in order to persuade people to be hopeful	Seeks evidence of the power of faith to help people rise above the pressures and problems of daily life
	Mystic	**Servant**	**Crusader**
Director	Prays for the needs of others through regular spiritual discipline	Extends tangible help to people in need in order to provide hope and encouragement	Organizes the proclamation of the Christian message as one of hope and possibility for the world
Dreamer	Prays for the realization of the kingdom of God and for the healing and happiness of all people	Tackles large and enduring problems with the hope of making change; pursues hope through institutional transformation	Paints hopeful pictures of what the world might become were the kingdom of God to come upon the earth and works toward that end
Pleaser	Lives in the personal belief that God will take care of all problems and that through prayer God will touch the lives of those in need	Makes personal contact and shares tangible help in order to care for and encourage those in need	Focuses on the Christian life as a means to happiness, wholeness, and fulfillment
Thinker	Practices deeply personal and private spiritual discipline, praying for hope, help, and healing in the community and the world	Organizes programs and practices of caregiving and help in order to create hope	Creates resources that others use to communicate hope, encouragement, and the promise of blessing

FAITH		
	Head	**Heart**	**Pilgrim**
Director	Provides a reasoned argument for why we should believe and what the benefits will be	Provides a passionate argument for why we should believe and what the benefits will be	While questioning specifics, has an unbounded confidence in the reality of a divine truth
Dreamer	Focuses on understanding the ways that faith affects life and how to maximize the benefits of faith	Focuses on how faith changes our life experiences and how faith makes life better	Creates settings where people can explore the great stories of the Christian life
Pleaser	Experiences faith as a "feel-good" power to enable the individual to live a more balanced life	Ignores what seems to be true and holds to what he or she believes God will do; not concerned with appearances	Interested in sharing beliefs, Christian or otherwise; wants to know why and how what we believe has power to change our lives
Thinker	Experiences faith as a formal, critical process of making sense of the world by coming to an academic understanding of God and God's power	Experiences faith as a contemplative activity that means what we believe much more than it means what we do	Explores the thinking of Christian authors, mystics, crusaders, saints, preachers, and so forth to gain deep insight into the full spectrum of Christian belief
	Mystic	**Servant**	**Crusader**
Director	Engages in intensive spiritual disciplines of prayer, fasting, contemplation, and study	Lives out faith in action through serving the needs of others in the name of Jesus Christ	Takes the faith of Jesus Christ to the masses, as Billy Graham does
Dreamer	Seeks God's presence in daily life and lives in a sense of spiritual empowerment	Lives in the assurance that God will provide for material needs while he or she serves out in the world	Finds ways to make every aspect of life an issue of faith; God is present in every act and decision, every event and occurrence
Pleaser	Experiences faith as a good feeling that God is present and active in the daily life	Convinced that faith leads to action and, in fact, that faith without works is worse than dead; feels that doing is more important than believing	Makes the Christian faith a paradise of blessing and good will; communicates the best of what it means to be Christian
Thinker	Engages in intensive spiritual disciplines of prayer, fasting, contemplation, and study	Experiences faith as the prime motivator to move out in service in the world	Writes and communicates messages of Christian apology and theology

GIVING		
	Head	**Heart**	**Pilgrim**

	Head	**Heart**	**Pilgrim**
Director	Defines giving financially, as a formal, reasoned process rather than a faith process	Defines giving more holistically, including time, talent, and money and as a response more emotional than rational	May be motivated by personal faith to give and raise funds for a variety of needs both Christian and nonreligious
Dreamer	Sees giving as a way of fulfilling Christian mission and service; wants to give to things that are meaningful	Gives from the heart to the things that matter most; doesn't want to give to mundane things, but to things of lasting significance	Gives or raises money to meet the needs of the moment; tries to do as much as possible with whatever is at hand
Pleaser	Moves toward goals for giving more, usually trying to increase financial giving by set amounts or percentages each year	Gives whatever he or she can whenever he or she can; usually wants to support every good cause	Often gives as a way to discover generosity rather than being motivated by generosity; understands giving as a way of learning about faith
Thinker	Creates a giving plan including amounts, schedules, and objectives; usually treats giving as limited to money	Devotes time, energy, and money to one or two causes that mean the most to her or him	May help others understand how giving can help them grow in the faith; good at organizing campaigns and appeals
	Mystic	**Servant**	**Crusader**
Director	Gives gifts anonymously and quietly; usually sees giving as a spiritual discipline	Sees sacrificial giving more as commitment of time, talent, and energy in service to others and less as related to money	Will set audacious financial goals and organize whatever processes are necessary to give or raise necessary funds
Dreamer	Sees giving as a way to put faith into action, usually in the area of money more than time and talent	Believes that there are no limits to what the individual ought to be willing to give to transform lives and the world	Creates motivational visions for the good that money can do in the name of God; often generous personally, also challenges the generosity of others
Pleaser	Prayerfully considers what to give and then finds specific outlets for giving to others	Likes to give money, gifts, and service to help, please, and comfort others	Generally ties giving into receiving blessing, reward, or a prize; giving is often tied to getting
Thinker	Understands giving as a personal and private expression of Christian devotion and an important aspect of spiritual discipline	Displays single-minded devotion to giving all to a specific cause or concern	Will create impressive systems and structures for channeling funds to important work

HEALING			
	Head	**Heart**	**Pilgrim**
Director	Develops a plan and process for extending healing to others; usually employs words and intercessory prayers	Responds to the needs of others in a case-by-case manner; usually employs touch and contact	Concerned with the healing of the heart as well as the body and soul
Dreamer	Uses a broad-based approach to healing, beyond the physical, centered in prayer, visitation, and reading and discussion	Uses a broad-based approach to healing, beyond the physical, centered in one-on-one contact, sharing experiences, and prayer	Open to both traditional and alternative methods of healing, including folk remedies, acupuncture, macrobiotics, and so forth
Pleaser	Talks about the healing power of Christ and the Christian faith and offers a reasoned argument for why believing leads to healing	Offers random, and not-so-random, acts of kindness with belief that actions speak louder than words	Approaches healing from the perspective of positive attitude and the power of the mind to heal the body
Thinker	Develops plans and programs for healing processes within a group or community; provides strong rationale for healing	Feels and thinks very deeply about the hurts and needs of the world; deals with healing issues one person at a time	Studies a variety of ways to heal body, mind, and spirit and emphasizes preventative rather than restorative cures
	Mystic	**Servant**	**Crusader**
Director	Extends the healing of God through prayer, visitation, and laying on of hands	Goes to places of hurt, need, and disease to offer prayer, comfort, and physical ministrations	Develops programs and services of healing and wholeness for those in need
Dreamer	Prays for the healing of the body, mind, and spirit of individuals, groups, families, communities, and the world	Works in hospice, hospital, nursing-care facilities, and so forth to extend the healing hands of Christ in the world	Often focuses on healing in one specific area or on the eradication of one particular condition or disease
Pleaser	Prays for individuals and communicates that prayers are being offered; healing is a central focus of the prayer life	Works in hospice, hospital, nursing-care facilities, and so forth to extend the healing hands of Christ in the world	Acts with an unswerving positive attitude so that healing becomes as contagious as disease
Thinker	Prays for the healing of the body, mind, and spirit of individuals, groups, families, communities, and the world	Develops a personal strategy for healing in a focused, limited way; pursues a single-minded devotion to a healing ministry	Generates massive amounts of information and focuses on a specific problem, disease, or crisis

	HELPING		
	Head	**Heart**	**Pilgrim**
Director	Designs a program for assisting with the work of others; usually adopts a specific role of offering a particular kind of help	Commits to offering help to the work of others; usually seeks to find out what help is needed, then works to provide it	Seeks to bring people from various backgrounds together to help make something large and wonderful happen; a helper of helpers
Dreamer	Offers support to front-line workers in ministry and service; generates ideas to help others	Makes regular offers to help and generates ideas to strengthen and support the work of others	Will gladly join in to help with groups and people who are not well known, where relationships are yet to be formed
Pleaser	Offers structured, formal help to the work of others; usually in the form of organizing or monitoring processes	Offers to do whatever is needed to assist with the work of others; has heartfelt desire to be helpful and take pressure off of others	Always ready to lend a hand to anyone who asks, unconstrained by denomination, faith tradition, or creed; doesn't help Christians only
Thinker	Provides detailed processes for getting work accomplished effectively; will attend to the detail work of most tasks	Provides perspective on what is needed to get the job done; particularly focuses on the needs of leaders	Creative in generating ideas of how people can be helped and what kinds of resources may be needed
	Mystic	**Servant**	**Crusader**
Director	Views helping as providing a spiritual centering for the work that needs to be done; serves the needs of others anonymously	Enters into a specific relationship of helping, usually behind the scenes, to make a particular service more effective	Organizes people around the needs of a central task or ministry and attends to all the details for staff and workers
Dreamer	Will generally write down ideas to help others grow in faith and to offer guidance to those who are in leadership	Enters into a variety of helping relationships with different people pursuing different tasks; "jack-of-all-trades"	Will generate elaborate plans for ways many people can serve in different jobs to make something big happen
Pleaser	Prays for the work of others and offers great moral support to others who work; often serves as personal counselor to those who lead	Makes a commitment to "be there" for people in need; will dedicate time and energy to providing assistance to leadership	Generally willing to help whoever is deemed worthy of help, but no one else; if the focus is on the hungry, won't attend to the homeless, and so forth
Thinker	Prays for the needs of those in leadership; deeply contemplates ways he or she can be in helpful service	Helps by critically analyzing all aspects of a project or process; "covers all the bases"; makes sure everything needed is available	Will create the how-to manual to get specific tasks, jobs, or ministries accomplished; generally has all the answers for particular tasks

INTERPRETATION OF TONGUES		
	Head	**Heart**	**Pilgrim**
Director	Interprets the speaking of other tongues and cultures to teach others the meaning and understanding of various concepts	Interprets the speaking of other tongues and cultures to inspire others by the faith witness shared	Helps people understand the common language spoken by people of different cultures, generations, and faith traditions
Dreamer	Uses gift to build community and confirm belief in God through bridging cultural/language differences	Witnesses to the presence of the Holy Spirit through the sharing of spiritual truth as held in common across cultural boundaries	Able to bring messages from secular sources to bear upon questions of faith for Christians and non-Christians alike
Pleaser	Interprets other languages as a way of building community and connecting with people different from her or his own group	Feels that interpretation builds individual relationships and enables different peoples to communicate and connect	Opens dialogue with non-Christians to find common images, thoughts, and ideas
Thinker	Regards interpretation as a way of deepening understanding and gaining information for the strengthening of faith	Sees interpretation as a way of deepening relationships with others who can share stories that deepen understanding and faith	Studies the messages of non-Christian groups with the intention of building bridges between Christianity and other ways of thinking
	Mystic	**Servant**	**Crusader**
Director	Interprets the speaking of other tongues in order to deepen the spiritual practices of others	Interprets the speaking of other tongues and cultures to build community and serve the needs of other people	Finds a common ground for understanding what people are saying about their faith and their relationship with Jesus Christ
Dreamer	Interprets tongues for personal growth and edification in order to better communicate the gospel to others	Feels that interpretation creates confidence in the universality of God's truth and inspires service to other cultures/groups	Seeks ways to align the messages of other traditions and cultures with the gospel of Jesus Christ
Pleaser	Interprets other languages as a way of hearing the voice of God in new ways to share with others	Interprets other languages as a means of serving the needs of others; sees interpretation as an act of service in and of itself	Connects the imagery of Christianity with the symbols and signs of other traditions in nonthreatening, nonjudgmental ways
Thinker	Sees interpretation as a personal means of receiving confirmation of God and understanding across cultural barriers	Interprets other languages as a way of gaining insight into what others believe and need to help define types of service	Listens deeply to the customs and practices of non-Christians to find ways to communicate the gospel of Jesus Christ

KNOWLEDGE		
	Head	**Heart**	**Pilgrim**
Director	Has intellectual approach to faith; gains information in order to provide a rational, academic argument for believing in God	Sees knowledge as a means to the end of faith and relationship building; believes that one knows what the Bible says in order to apply it to life	Has great passion for learning about all faith traditions and ready retention of similarities and differences
Dreamer	Finds that knowledge generates ideas and creative thinking and stimulates growth through the sharing of information and teaching	Experiences knowledge as leading us to deep thinking and processing of information for application to real-life situations	Able to translate academic information into symbolic and esoteric language
Pleaser	Uses knowledge as a way of establishing harmony and peace and sharing faith with others; seeks extremely practical applications	Uses knowledge as a basis for building interpersonal relationships; believes learning involves making life better for others	Uses broad grasp of concepts and ideas to make people feel good about their own learning and development
Thinker	Engages in academic pursuit of information to prove the truth of God; sees knowledge as the foundation upon which faith is based	Sees knowledge as leading to a deeper relationship with Jesus Christ; believes the more we understand, the more faithful we are	Develops an ever-deepening understanding and appreciation of spiritual and theological ideas
	Mystic	**Servant**	**Crusader**
Director	Believes knowledge gives us deeper understanding of God so that we can explain God to others, usually one-on-one	Sees knowledge as a tool necessary to know what to do, how to do it, and how to be most effective in service to others	Believes that vast understanding of the major body of information is necessary to perform specific tasks and ministries
Dreamer	Uses knowledge of God and knowledge of truth to find deeper levels of relationship and to provide guidance to others	Uses knowledge to open the possibilities for service and sharing in the name of Christ; applies know-how to practical situations	Able to adapt concrete knowledge into abstract concepts, and vice versa
Pleaser	Defines knowledge as knowledge of God and an assurance of God's presence in the world; feels that head knowledge feeds the soul	Sees knowledge as a means to the end of being able to serve more effectively in the world	Uses knowledge to empower people for the accomplishment of important work and ministry
Thinker	Follows deeply contemplative approach to faith; reads Christian mystical classics to provide confirmation of the efficacy of spiritual discipline	Sees knowledge as power and as giving the servant an advantage in the world; thinks knowledge "levels the playing field"	Concentrates on deepening and broadening the grasp of information and ideas necessary to perform a specific goal or ministry

LEADERSHIP		
	Head	**Heart**	**Pilgrim**
Director	Leads by developing, directing, and implementing a plan; usually persuasive in word and action; primarily leads alone	Leads by pursuing a compelling vision; communicates with passion, emotion, and conviction; primarily leads alone	Able to inspire people with a variety of differing spiritual approaches to work together to seek truth and understanding
Dreamer	Details elaborate plans for growth and success; develops new, innovative programs; good at long-range planning; thinks about big picture	Innovative, creative, and always asking "what if" kinds of questions; adopts "the sky's the limit" attitude; has lots of energy	Has visions for spiritual growth and development that transcend different approaches to create a safe environment for exploration and questioning
Pleaser	Builds community and fellowship by developing structures and systems; highly organized around issues involving people	More of a family head than an organizational head; leads people toward a better future; always keeps their best interests in mind	Has a collaborative approach to leadership, engaging vast numbers of people in accomplishing tasks and exploring possibilities
Thinker	Writes the proposals, manuals, and guidelines which others follow; good at defining the rules and developing effective structures	Writes the personnel policies; enjoys conducting job evaluations; helpful in determining best way for people to move forward	Creates resources to help leaders be effective in diverse and culturally mixed settings
	Mystic	**Servant**	**Crusader**
Director	Leads a group of spiritual seekers in practicing disciplines; often aims at forming community rather than serving other needs	Leads efforts to serve others, to accomplish tasks, and to develop structures for Christian service	Enabled by charismatic force to mobilize groups toward the common end
Dreamer	A guru; usually introspective and aloof; has insight that is sought out and put into practice by others	Charismatic and intense in devotion to a cause; appears unswerving in focus; visionary; often a lone ranger	Has compelling vision of promised-land destinations that motivate entire communities of people
Pleaser	Heads a community or small group of spiritual seekers; provides a safe place for spiritual growth and direction	Serves with a single devotion to making life better and richer for others; often a lone ranger	Motivates people to enjoy doing hard and monumental tasks
Thinker	Writes the devotionals and guidelines for spiritual discipline and direction; offers instruction to others based in experience	Organizes others to action and service based in a clarity of understanding about needs and ways to fulfill needs	Develops effective theory and practice for leaders who are committed to specific tasks and ministries

MIRACLES		
	Head	**Heart**	**Pilgrim**

	Head	**Heart**	**Pilgrim**
Director	Operates from and communicates a rational argument for reality of miracles in the world; points out the miraculous in the common	Communicates the miraculous with passion and conviction; prays for the miracles to be experienced or recognized by others	Seeks the miraculous in the world as a way of answering questions of faith; sees miracles as evidence that proves a divine power
Dreamer	Seeks the miraculous in the ordinary; always looking at life through eyes of one who expects miracles; believes miracles make sense	Seeks the miraculous in the ordinary; has faith bolstered by the miracles that are found; "knows" miracles happen by faith	Holds a vision for a time when the miraculous is commonplace and the spiritual power of our faith is in evidence
Pleaser	Visitation warrior who goes to those in need with a message of God's miraculous and healing love; is in close affinity with servant	Feels miracles need no explanation—that's why they're miracles; considers understanding not as important as belief; feels miracles give hope	Shares evidence of miracles as a source of hope, encouragement, and proof of the presence of the divine
Thinker	Usually attempts to remove the miracle from the miraculous; creates detailed arguments and explanations for why miracles make sense	Creates detailed arguments for the truth of miracles in our day; illustrates the miraculous through personal experience.	Delves deeply into the meaning of the miraculous, and shares reasoned, open-minded explanations with others
	Mystic	**Servant**	**Crusader**
Director	Prays for miracles and interprets the miracles of God to others; holds the historic tradition of miracles as confirmation	Holds that the miracles of God are performed through human hands; extends gift of miracles to those in need	Often will base the entire focus of a ministry or program around belief in or evidence of miracles
Dreamer	Sees all of life as a miracle and counsels others to participate in the miracle; has very strong belief in laying on hands and in prayer	Feels compelled to take the miracles of God into the world; has no doubt that God's power can save and transform; has strong zeal and determination	May commit to creating the experience of miracles for others in the form of faith healings, reconciliation, or exorcisms
Pleaser	Sees miracles as a source of comfort, hope, and joy; uses miracles to create a deep foundation of faith; urges community to continuously pray for miracles	Offers the healing, empowering energy of God to all; expects miracles to bring comfort and hope to the afflicted	Presents miracles as a source of comfort, a proof of God's activity in the world and a motivation for conversion to the Christian faith
Thinker	Deeply introspective; sees miracles as a personal confirmation of the power and presence of God in the world; shares validation with others	Finds miracles to be a motivation to serve and a way of using God's power to make life better for others	Spends time seeking miraculous stories and experiences that support and confirm his or her commitment to ministry

PROPHECY			
	Head	**Heart**	**Pilgrim**
Director	Proclaims intense, well-structured, highly reasonable messages to convince believers and nonbelievers alike to offer deeper commitment	Proclaims impassioned messages that convey an urgency to move toward a deeper commitment to Jesus Christ	Leads studies and discussions on revelations of God's will and explorations of the best way to respond to the message
Dreamer	Proclaims messages of deep commitment to Jesus Christ using rich visual imagery and compelling visionary language	Proclaims messages of repentance and commitment to Jesus Christ using visual and emotionally charged language	Holds a vision from God that is shared in a variety of ways, taking into account the cultural context and varied experience of the people
Pleaser	Proclaims messages of need for commitment and repentance from a position of concern for the individual	Proclaims urgent messages of need for repentance and commitment for the good of the individual	Gives considerable time to people to share a revealed message or vision to make sure they adopt it as their own
Thinker	Thinks and writes on theological matters; develops systematic messages that explain the will of God for our world	Writes or thinks on theological and devotional matters; provides messages of repentance and hope	Writes about and communicates comparative religious ideas that focus on a single issue or message
	Mystic	**Servant**	**Crusader**
Director	Provides balanced and calm counsel to individuals and groups to move to deeper commitment to Jesus Christ	Proclaims impassioned messages that convey an urgency to move to deeper commitment to those outside the church in the world	Has a clear and definite message to relay to each and every person encountered
Dreamer	Provides a vision for community in Christ and union with Christ to individuals and small groups; prays for God's vision to be revealed	Street-corner preacher, caught in the fervor to proclaim the word of God out in the world, calling for repentance and commitment	Has single-minded devotion to proclaiming a God-given vision for a particular group of people
Pleaser	Provides balanced and calm counsel to individuals and groups, with emphasis on the benefits of repentance and deep commitment	Proclaims impassioned messages of repentance and belief in hopes of bringing comfort and hope to others in the world	Has commitment to proclaim a message, usually of hope, comfort, peace, and encouragement
Thinker	Thinks and writes on devotional matters; provides reflection information for others on the journey of faith	Organizes work and movements to spread the message of repentance and commitment to the world	Works as author or speaker developing and deepening her or his message around a single theme or idea

132

SERVANTHOOD		
	Head	**Heart**	**Pilgrim**
Director	Develops thorough and comprehensive programs and processes to serve the needs of others	Commits to lead programs and processes designed to serve the needs of others	Seeks to meet the needs of as many people as possible, whether they subscribe to Christianity or not
Dreamer	Develops many different systems and processes to serve the needs of others in a variety of ways	Serves, in many different ways, many different individuals or groups of people; follows the shifting movements of the heart	Generates service ideas for a church or organization that meet the specified needs in an area
Pleaser	Serves in order to bring comfort and aid to those with greatest need; considers message of gospel not as important as modeling gospel	Serves in order to fulfill need to do for others and to grow in personal faith and discipleship	Has dedication to serving the comfort needs of others; strives to transform difficult circumstances into stress-free environments
Thinker	Provides descriptions for authentic servant leaders; is focused on the details necessary for effective service to be rendered by self and others	Moves into the world in order to serve the needs of others; speaks words of support and assurance as much as rendering tangible service	Studies the example of servant leaders in a variety of spiritual traditions through history to generate models of servanthood
	Mystic	**Servant**	**Crusader**
Director	Dedicated to Christian service in the world without desire for recognition or reward	Leader or follower committed to serving the needs of others wherever those needs are found in the world	Dedicates life to serving the needs of a particular group or region
Dreamer	Serves the needs of an individual or small group with passion and total devotion	Serves, in many different ways, many different individuals or groups of people; follows the shifting movements of the heart	Has great desire to save the world one person at a time, one day at a time
Pleaser	Serves with a total and complete devotion to meeting the material and spiritual needs of others	Has intense desire to serve others in order to give hope, comfort, and happiness; highly committed to action	Holds a strong vision for making people happy through meeting their fundamental physical, emotional, and spiritual needs
Thinker	Serves the spiritual needs of other Christian pilgrims seeking God; offers passive service where faith needs rather than material needs are met	Organizes the work of self and others to provide meaningful, tangible service to others; focused on works rather than faith	Gathers together information, resources, and tools necessary to be effective in serving a group or region

SHEPHERDING			
	Head	**Heart**	**Pilgrim**
Director	Provides mentoring to another individual, mentoring that is intellectual and based in study and discussion	Provides mentoring to another individual, mentoring that is relational and based in experiences, feelings, and stories	Journeys with another seeker through the questions, doubts, hopes, and confusions of faith development
Dreamer	Provides mentoring to others in ways of thinking, believing, and learning; focuses on knowing God	Provides mentoring to others in ways of relating, believing, and caring; focuses on building relationship with God and neighbor	Works with other seekers to explore and interpret spiritual visions to help address the questions of faith
Pleaser	Provides mentoring to others as a way of helping them grow in their discipleship and make their lives more fulfilling	Provides mentoring to others as a way of helping them experience God in deep ways so that their lives might be more fulfilling	Works with individuals to find the benefits of the spiritual life for improving and deepening the faith
Thinker	Provides mentoring to another individual, mentoring that is intellectual and based in study and discussion	Provides mentoring to others in ways of feeling, relating to God and others by appealing to both emotion and reason	Creates guidelines and instructions for others to use to explore their faith and provides ongoing feedback and counsel
	Mystic	**Servant**	**Crusader**
Director	Provides mentoring to another individual; intuitive and inward-focused; aimed toward spiritual discipline and faith formation	Provides mentoring to another individual by example, leading others into faith-in-action; teaches practical skills for service	Takes on the role of guide or spiritual director to lead a disciple into a lifelong ministry or mission focus
Dreamer	Provides mentoring to others in spiritual/experiential practices; cultivates disciples	Provides mentoring to others through example and teaching; feels great desire to save the world one person at a time	Focuses attention on sharing a vision for ministry with another individual or small group
Pleaser	Provides mentoring to others to deepen their spiritual center and transform their experience of God	Provides mentoring to others as a way of serving both the needs of the mentored and those further served	Works with individuals or small groups to equip them to carry on specific ministries and tasks
Thinker	Provides mentoring to another individual, often in the form of spiritual direction; focused on deepening relationship to God	Provides mentoring, usually to an individual, to help train another to serve in the world	Acts as a spiritual guide for an individual who is embarking on a specific, narrowly focused mission or ministry

TEACHING		
	Head	**Heart**	**Pilgrim**
Director	Teaches others relying on information, facts, and figures to facilitate learning; highly intellectual	Teaches others relying on experience, stories, and feelings; highly relational	Teaches a broad spectrum of great religious and spiritual thought to help people find what they truly believe
Dreamer	Teaches others using abstract concepts, theories, and ideas; highly stimulating, but also intellectual	Teaches others using vision language, symbols, and metaphor; highly esoteric	Loves ideas and creates opportunities for people to examine concepts from a variety of perspectives and learning styles
Pleaser	Teaches using information, ideas, and facts that convey the benefit of believing and ways to personally improve	Teaches others using stories, experiences, and feelings in order to provide assurance and strengthening of the individual's faith	Adopts an open approach to learning that blends fun, discovery, and information gathering with critical thinking
Thinker	Teaches using words, concepts, ideas, information, reasoning, and theory; ultra-intellectual	Teaches using feelings, hunches, theories, intuitions, stories, parables, and so forth; blends emotion and reason	Develops open and broad-based curriculum for other teachers; gains greatest satisfaction from teaching teachers
	Mystic	**Servant**	**Crusader**
Director	Teaches others relying on spiritual discipline, experience, and intuition; highly devotional	Teaches others relying on hands-on experiences and other learn-by-doing methods; uses "high-touch" interaction	Effectively communicates information and knowledge needed to be effective in spreading the gospel of Jesus Christ
Dreamer	Teaches others relying on spiritual language and practice; highly symbolic and transcendent	Teaches others by example and involvement in a variety of different kinds of service	Shares a comprehensive approach to a particular theme or concept needed to carry out effective ministry
Pleaser	Teaches others through spiritual practice how to experience affective union with Christ in all times and places	Teaches others by example in order to serve both those others and the world	Uses humor and interaction to share a comprehensive body of information for successful ministry
Thinker	Teaches using complex thinking of deep spiritual matters; applies discussion and reason to transcendent matters	Teaches others by instructing them in the best ways to channel efforts and energy to the completion of certain tasks	Develops comprehensive and detailed instructions and information for the effective accomplishment of specific tasks or ministries

TONGUES		
	Head	**Heart**	**Pilgrim**
Director	Speaks in foreign languages in order to communicate the gospel of Jesus Christ	Speaks in foreign languages in order to help people come to know God in a personal way	Invites conversation with a variety of languages to investigate the way that deep spiritual truths are communicated
Dreamer	Speaks in foreign languages in order to share God's vision for another people in another place	Speaks in a foreign language in order to excite and inspire others by the power of God to transcend limits of speech and culture	Uses the language and symbols of other cultures to create inspirational messages
Pleaser	Speaks in a foreign language to communicate the gospel of Jesus Christ as a confirmation of the truth of God	Speaks in a foreign language to build community and give hope and comfort to people of other cultures	Uses a God-given language to create community, build trust, and forge ongoing relationships
Thinker	Speaks in a foreign language to communicate ideas, information, and concepts about God to other cultures	Speaks in a foreign language to tell stories and communicate experiences of faith to foreigners in order to convince them of the truth of Christ	Studies the patterns and practices of another culture in whose language he or she is able to communicate
	Mystic	**Servant**	**Crusader**
Director	Speaks in foreign languages as a form of devotional worship to build faith in the community	Speaks in foreign languages in order to communicate with people in different places to offer aid and comfort	Commits to communicating the gospel in one specific God-given language
Dreamer	Speaks in a foreign language in order to communicate the spiritual reality of God to people of other cultures	Speaks in a foreign language in order to inspire others to service by convincing them of the power of God	Speaks in visionary language to a foreign group or culture
Pleaser	Speaks in a foreign language to instruct spiritual pilgrims in their devotional lives	Speaks in a foreign language in order to serve the needs of others and give comfort and aid in the name of Christ	Speaks the good news in a foreign language that helps people gain a vision for the future based in hope and blessing
Thinker	Speaks in a foreign tongue in order to educate pilgrims of other cultures in spiritual discipline	Speaks in a foreign language in order to mobilize foreigners to work together to serve in the name of Jesus Christ	Creates materials and resources in another language that promote the spreading of the gospel of Jesus Christ

WISDOM		
	Head	**Heart**	**Pilgrim**
Director	Relies upon reason and information to interpret life situations and make sense of the complexities of living as Christian disciples	Relies upon common sense and experience to interpret life situations and find God's presence in the day-to-day	Integrates meaning with information from a wide spectrum of religious teachings and spiritual writings
Dreamer	Relies upon intuition and reason to see order in chaos and solutions in the midst of problems; balanced	Knows that God is at work in the world and that no problem is so great that calm and balance cannot overcome it	Interprets visions, intuitions, and abstract ideas that help people understand the mysteries of faith
Pleaser	Shares life experiences and the life lessons learned as a way of being in ministry to the needs of others	Shares life experiences and personal parables to put life in perspective and help others see order in the chaotic	Acts as fount of comfort and reconciliation; interprets meaning from the day-to-day experiences within a community of disciples
Thinker	Provides rational, reasonable explanations for the intuitive, commonsense knowledge of real life	Provides stories and illustrations that prove the commonsense, intuitive knowledge of God's presence	Creates resources to help others better understand their Christian journey and the meaning of spiritual teachings and disciplines for the Christian life
	Mystic	**Servant**	**Crusader**
Director	Shares the observations and interpretations of daily life as a way of finding God's Spirit at work in the world	Shares experiences and intuitive knowledge as a basis for moving forward to serve in the world	Provides the experience and perspective necessary for ministries to be accomplished in the best way possible
Dreamer	Sees the implicit order in life and understands how God is at work in our lives	Shares experiences and hopes as a way of helping others understand the presence of God in the world	Interprets in a visionary way God's call to specific ministries, projects, and programs
Pleaser	Shares experience and understanding as a way of building spiritual community and faith formation	Shares the commonsense lessons of life with others as a ministry of healing and compassion; offers balance and perspective	Able to apply the lessons of the Bible and the history of the Christian church to current reality to strengthen the ministry or mission
Thinker	Deeply reflective of life experiences; uses rational explanations to better understand the more abstract forms of spiritual knowledge	Solves problems by taking what she or he has learned and applying it to the needs and issues of the world	Provides the definitive rationale and reasoning for focus on and commitment to a specific project, program, or ministry

Phase of Life Context

Our church is home to the whole spectrum of the Phase of Life context. Ministry to the various age groups requires a clear understanding of what each is seeking and what each has to offer.

Early Childhood: Birth to 7 Years. Children need to be received as full members of the community of faith. The most important ministry to this age group is to help them experience the church as a good place to be. Fellowship, education, and worship should all be designed to fit their level of learning.

Childhood: 8–12. This group needs activity. Put these older children to work helping others, serving the community, and understanding the call to serve that comes from the gospel. Where there is meaningful service, older children stay interested. Don't forget to play.

Youth: 13–18. Missional service is even more important now. Give the youth something to do. Then help them understand how their service fulfills the gospel. Don't be afraid to get serious with youth about prayer, reading the Bible, fasting, worship, and service. They're more ready than we sometimes give them credit for.

Young Adult: 19–26. Instead of seeing people this age as a problem to be solved, talk to them. Ask them what they need, don't tell them what they ought to have. Help them find out who God wants them to be. Link them in small groups with others who ask the same questions. Don't make them feel like outsiders. Give them their own leadership responsibilities for the church they want to develop.

Starter: 27–39. Ask not what this group can do for the church; ask what the church can do for this group. This age has the greatest demands on time, money, energy, and relationships. They need the church to help them find balance, purpose, and understanding. The more the church offers them in the way of comfort and healing at this stage of life, the more likely they are to stay in the church and give something back when the kids leave the nest and they have more disposable time, energy, and money. No other age group has experienced the stress that this group confronts today, and the church has a very special and important ministry to married people and singles in this phase of life.

Midlife: 40–59. Boomers abound, and they will redefine the way the world works as they come to power in this decade. This age group will bring massive change in and through the church. This is the most highly educated, professionally trained group ever in the history of the church. They are calling for a more sophisticated educational opportunity, more interesting, professionally conducted worship, high-quality fellowship experiences, and professionally run organizational systems in the church. This is a demanding group, but they are willing to put their money and time where their mouths are. There could be a power struggle for the next ten years as this group comes to dominance in the leadership of the church.

Transition: 60–72. This group is experiencing a fundamental change of life—moving from work to retirement. Many are relocating to a different part of the country. People in the transition phase have low denominational loyalty, and they are as interested in being ministered to as they are willing to be in ministry to others. They are used to solving problems with money, but now money is a more limited, finite resource. They will invest in the things that have the greatest meaning. If the church wants their time and money, it must be faithful to use it well, both to serve the institution and also to serve the people. This group wants meaningful work to do; thus, this age group is the most active in Habitat for Humanity projects and is least interested in serving on committees.

Older Adult: 73–??. The backbone of the church for the past thirty years, this group is moving deeper into retirement, and they are hanging up their gloves in the church as well. This group is needing to be ministered to, but they are very much still a force to be reckoned with. They are interested in churches that will offer them community and a wide variety of programs that help them to be Christian. Fellowship moves to the fore, and they are looking for traditional worship and education experiences that give comfort, hope, and stability.

Follow-Up Exercises

Download handouts from www.equippedforeverygoodwork.org

MATERIALS

pencils

writing surface
(table groupings are best)

HANDOUTS

Questions for Reflection

Spiritual Gifts Bingo

Activating the Spirituality
Web Through the Means
of Grace

Spirituality Web Scripture
Exploration

Designing Teams
for Effective Ministry

QUESTIONS FOR REFLECTION

This material is intended for use in following up on the discovery process. At least one follow-up gathering should be planned before the group disbands. In preparation for the work that will continue, and as a means of summarizing what has been learned, lead the group through the "Questions for Reflection" exercise.

First: Distribute the "Questions for Reflection" worksheet and give participants 10-15 minutes to respond to and reflect on these questions:

- What have you learned about yourself from this process?
- What has been confirmed? What was surprising?
- How will you use what you have learned?
- How do your Spiritual Gifts, Leadership/Interaction Style, Spirituality Type, and Task Type relate to your desires and God's will for you?

Second: Give participants five minutes to talk about their responses, one-on-one, each with another participant.

Third: Have each "listener" report what was heard to the larger group.

Taking time to record insights before leaving the group setting helps to make them more real. Talking about insights with another person and knowing you have been truly heard provides a sense of value and connection.

SPIRITUAL GIFTS BINGO

At a follow-up gathering, play Spiritual Gifts Bingo.

Recognizing our gifts in the lives of Biblical characters is a good way to broaden dialogue about the nature and understanding of our giftedness. All twenty gifts are listed among the five different sheets. Distribute copies of the sheets to different groups and provide some time for them to research and discuss their findings. Then share discoveries in the larger group.

Spiritual Gifts Bingo

Find biblical characters who you feel possess the gifts on this sheet. Use a different character for each square. Be sure you can explain why each character you choose fits that particular gift. When you (or your team) complete the sheet, turn it in to the group leader.

Shepherding	Helping	Evangelism
Interpretation of Tongues	Any Gift *Jesus Christ* Free Space	Wisdom
Administration	Leadership	Giving

LEADERSHIP/INTERACTION STYLES (LIS) GROUP EXERCISE

When time permits, do this group exercise to further explore the Leadership/Interaction Styles. There may be individuals who are behaving out of a particular style because it is dominant in the group. This exercise can help reveal how someone may be blocked from living out of her or his own style. It is also a graphic way to illustrate what it feels like to be in the minority. A lone Dreamer in a group of Directors can feel like a real outcast.

Group people together by their Leadership/Interaction Styles. Have them list three advantages and three disadvantages to their style. Then, in the larger group, talk about the insights and consider together what the implications are of balance (or imbalance) among the four styles.

ACTIVATING THE SPIRITUALITY WEB THROUGH THE MEANS OF GRACE

Test your understanding of the Spirituality Web. As the Week of Prayer for Christian Unity approaches, what would your actions or attitudes be if you encounter God through Pilgrim spirituality? How would you prepare? How would you participate? How would that be different for the other types?

Walk a spiritual mile in one another's shoes. Complete the exercise for each of the illustrations shown.

Prayer: Week of Prayer for Christian Unity

Head: _____

Heart: _____

Pilgrim: _____

Mystic: _____

Servant: _____

Crusader: _____

Study: Tuesday Evening Bible Study

Head: _____

Heart: _____

Pilgrim: _____

Mystic: _____

Servant: _____

Crusader: _____

Lord's Supper: Communion Service

    Head: _____

    Heart: _____

    Pilgrim: _____

    Mystic: _____

    Servant: _____

    Crusader: _____

Fasting/Abstinence: Lent

    Head: _____

    Heart: _____

    Pilgrim: _____

    Mystic: _____

    Servant: _____

    Crusader: _____

Christian Conference: Small Group at an All-Church Retreat

    Head: _____

    Heart: _____

    Pilgrim: _____

    Mystic: _____

    Servant: _____

    Crusader: _____

Acts of Mercy: Food Bank

    Head: _____

    Heart: _____

    Pilgrim: _____

    Mystic: _____

    Servant: _____

    Crusader: _____

SPIRITUALITY WEB SCRIPTURE EXPLORATION EXERCISE

When time permits, perhaps in a follow-up gathering, do the Scripture Exploration Exercise. One suggested passage is John 15:1-17, or you may use one of your own choosing. You will need to prepare some comments about the context for #2. Imagine. When and where does the event take place? Who is speaking, who is listening?

Be sure to follow the exercise with group discussion about the experience. A strong appreciation of our different approaches and experiences of God can emerge through this exercise.

Scripture Exploration Exercise

Using the horizontal and vertical poles of the Spirituality Wheel that Corinne Ware adapted from Urban Holmes,[1] this exercise provides four different ways to study and pray a passage of Scripture. It will show you approaches and experiences of the holy different from your own. There is joy in each; using all four for one passage provides a rich experience and will almost certainly deepen your understanding of the passage. Establish a quiet, comfortable environment. Participants may find it helpful to write down their responses.

1. Feel It: Read the passage aloud. Is there anything in this passage that makes you angry, afraid, sad, or especially joyful? Write down or draw your responses.

2. Imagine It: As you read the passage a second time, silently, try to place yourself in the setting. Imagine you are one of the apostles or a new believer. What do your clothes feel like on your body? What foods are on the table? Who else is there? What do they look like? What do you smell, hear, taste, and see?

3. Think About It: Read the passage again. Why do you think this passage was written and included in Scripture? What is significant in this passage for our lives today? What did it have to say to the first hearers and to us? Are they different answers? Why? What does it tell us about God? about human beings? about our relationship with God?

4. Meditate on It: Read the passage one more time silently. Then, put down your papers. Close your eyes. Take a few deep breaths. Empty your mind of any thoughts about the passage. Try to simply focus your attention on God and listen. If an impression or thought comes to you, acknowledge it, then refocus your attention on God. If you find day-to-day thoughts intruding, focus again on the passage and then let it go. After a time, open your eyes and stretch. You might want to record any impressions or thoughts that emerged from your meditation. If not, simply accept the gift you have given yourself of quiet time with God.

Now that you have had an opportunity to study the passage in four different ways, take a few moments to share your feelings and thoughts about the exercise itself. Was one approach more comfortable than the others? Did you find yourself resisting a particular approach? What was most valuable and/or most frustrating for you?

NOTES

1. See *Discover Your Spiritual Type: A Guide to Individual and Congregational Growth,* by Corinne Ware (Alban Institute, 1995), pages 7-9, 103-7; compare *A History of Christian Spirituality: An Analytical Introduction,* by Urban T. Holmes (Seabury, 1980), pages 3-5.

DESIGNING TEAMS FOR EFFECTIVE MINISTRY EXERCISE

Wesley United Methodist Church is seeking to redesign its ministries from a gifts base. They would like to concentrate on seven ministry areas, and they wish to maximize their effectiveness. Each ministry unit will require a team of leaders. The size of each team is six to eight members. No individual may serve on more than two teams. Using the information provided, work to design the seven ministry teams.

Name	Primary Gift	LIS	Spirituality Type	Task Type
Alan Anderson	Giving	Pleaser	Pilgrim	Fellowship
Beth Blass	Leadership	Director	Head	Project
Carol Crane	Faith	Thinker	Servant	Process
Dave Denny**	Administration	Pleaser	Head	Process
Evelyn Estes	Healing	Dreamer	Mystic	Fellowship
Faith Ford	Exhortation	Director	Crusader	Project
Gerald Gray	Knowledge	Thinker	Head	Project
Hank Hall	Teaching	Dreamer	Servant	Fellowship
Isaac Iverson	Shepherding	Director	Head	Work
Jane Jennings	Servanthood	Director	Servant	Project
Kay Kramer	Evangelism	Dreamer	Heart	Work
Linda Long	Miracles	Pleaser	Pilgrim	Fellowship
Mike Marshall	Leadership	Dreamer	Mystic	Project
Nancy Noonan	Faith	Director	Heart	Fellowship
Oscar O'Brien	Discernment	Pleaser	Head	Project
Penny Pratt	Healing	Pleaser	Heart	Fellowship
Quinn Quigley	Administration	Thinker	Head	Work
Randy Rogers	Wisdom	Director	Heart	Project
Sarah Scott*	Teaching	Pleaser	Servant	Fellowship
Tom Trainor	Prophecy	Director	Servant	Project
Ursula Updike	Apostleship	Dreamer	Heart	Work
Veronica Vale	Teaching	Pleaser	Mystic	Process
Wendell Wall	Giving	Thinker	Head	Process
Xander Xytl	Servanthood	Pleaser	Heart	Project
Yolanda Yves	Leadership	Director	Mystic	Fellowship
Zebulun Zook	Discernment	Thinker	Pilgrim	Process

*Sarah Scott is the senior pastor

**Dave Denny is the associate pastor

Ministry Area #1: Worship

Wesley United Methodist Church has decided to go to two Sunday services: one aimed at the older, established congregation and a new service targeting younger Baby Boomers and their families.

Ministry Area #2: Children's programming, including education

Wesley United Methodist Church has made children and children's issues a priority for the coming year. The current facility has many potential uses for daycare, Christian education, and family activities.

Ministry Area #3: Adult programming, including education

Wesley United Methodist Church has a long tradition of quality Christian education for adults and is interested in developing a community identity as a learning center.

Ministry Area #4: Ministry to older adults

Wesley United Methodist Church is strategically located near two retirement facilities, and almost 30 percent of its membership is at or above retirement age. Many members have expressed a desire to serve the older community.

Ministry Area #5: Food bank/soup kitchen development

Wesley United Methodist Church has received a large gift to be used to establish a food bank. Three members have made a commitment to donate funds and services to create a twice-weekly soup lunch for the poor and underprivileged in the area.

Ministry Area #6: Spiritual life development

Wesley United Methodist Church wants to provide more opportunity for members to explore spiritual discipline and faith formation experiences. Covenant groups, visitation teams, prayer groups, and spiritual direction are some alternatives to be examined.

Ministry Area #7: Stewardship

Wesley United Methodist Church is setting a priority on helping the congregation grow in their Christian faith through stewardship education. Spiritual giftedness, personal financial management, giving, and service will be the focuses of this process.

Spiritual Gifts Data

These sixteen tables reflect data collected between January 1990 and December 2000 primarily in United Methodist churches across the United States. Representatives from 3,672 congregations—white, African American, Caribbean Black, Hispanic, Korean, Japanese, Chinese, Cuban, Mexican American, Hmong, African, European, and South American—are comprised in the current sample. In addition, the sample reflects Presbyterian, Catholic, Assembly of God, parish nurse, healthcare worker, and Vanderbilt University administrator subgroups. Jurisdictionally, the congregational representation is as follows:

Northeastern	891	Western	593
Southeastern	801	North Central	571
South Central	718	Central Conferences	98

Twenty thousand eight hundred eighty-two (20,882) men and women[1] participated in the gifts discovery program. These results reflect responses to a self-report inventory of two hundred statements. The primary gift is the highest score on the inventory. Secondary gifts are the next three or four highest scores (in case of ties).

The majority of people surveyed were clergy and laity leadership in local congregations.[2] These results reflect not congregations as a whole but primarily the people in positions of leadership within the congregations.

The gifts represent relative scores reported on the survey. The survey defines spiritual giftedness as "gifts given by God that enable us to live spiritually empowered lives. Spiritual gifts are corporate in nature; given for the upbuilding of the body of Christ and the common good." Spiritual gifts are given not that people may be put on appropriate committees in the church but that we might live as faithful disciples in the world. This survey helps individuals better understand themselves as gifted people.

Tables 1 & 2: Primary and secondary gifts of all people surveyed
Tables 3 & 4: Primary and secondary gifts of surveyed laity
Tables 5 & 6: Primary and secondary gifts of surveyed clergy
Tables 7 & 8: Primary and secondary gifts of surveyed youth
Tables 9 & 10: Primary and secondary gifts of district superintendents
Tables 11 & 12: Primary and secondary gifts of males surveyed
Tables 13 & 14: Primary and secondary gifts of females surveyed
Table 15: Primary gifts by jurisdiction (including Central Conferences)
Table 16: Primary gifts among six separate constituencies

These findings are not statistically reliable, nor are they balanced regarding age, race/ethnicity, or gender. They are the cumulative results of over seven hundred spiritual gifts workshops with congregations, districts, and conferences within the United Methodist connection. No broad assertions can be drawn from any of the results reported. This material is presented simply for information and reflection.

<u>NOTES</u>

1. 12,044 women; 8,838 men (988 teenagers)
2. 3,648 clergy (2,517 male; 1,131 female); 17,234 laity (6,321 male; 10,913 female)

Spiritual Giftedness (Sample Size N=20,882) ranked by Primary Gift

		Primary Gift	Secondary Gift
1	Helping/Assistance	2429	5948
2	Faith	2167	6933
3	Healing	2093	6397
4	Teaching	1612	5142
5	Administration	1580	4343
6	Miracles	1572	4205
7	Knowledge	1336	4291
8	Servanthood	1320	3867
9	Shepherding	1304	4465
10	Giving	1053	3314
11	Exhortation	954	3190
12	Prophecy	835	3373
13	Leadership	748	4036
14	Discernment	739	1940
15	Evangelism	687	3170
16	Wisdom	549	2499
17	Compassion	525	1881
18	Apostleship	415	1277
19	Interpretation of Tongues	71	237
20	Tongues	44	99
		22,033	70,607

TABLE 1

Spiritual Giftedness (Sample Size N=20,882) ranked by Secondary Gift

		Primary Gift	Secondary Gift
1	Faith	2167	6933
2	Healing	2093	6397
3	Helping/Assistance	2429	5948
4	Teaching	1612	5142
5	Shepherding	1304	4465
6	Administration	1580	4343
7	Knowledge	1336	4291
8	Miracles	1572	4205
9	Leadership	748	4036
10	Servanthood	1320	3867
11	Prophecy	835	3373
12	Giving	1053	3314
13	Exhortation	954	3190
14	Evangelism	687	3170
15	Wisdom	549	2499
16	Discernment	739	1940
17	Compassion	525	1881
18	Apostleship	415	1277
19	Interpretation of Tongues	71	237
20	Tongues	44	99
		22,033	70,607

TABLE 2

Laity Spiritual Giftedness (Sample Size N=17,234) ranked by Primary Gift

		Primary Gift	Secondary Gift
1	Helping/Assistance	2160	5219
2	Faith	1871	5908
3	Healing	1776	5544
4	Miracles	1343	3360
5	Teaching	1323	4000
6	Administration	1321	3749
7	Knowledge	1049	3484
8	Servanthood	1040	2988
9	Shepherding	1025	3699
10	Giving	927	2872
11	Exhortation	778	2606
12	Discernment	644	1646
13	Prophecy	606	2477
14	Leadership	551	3497
15	Evangelism	522	2769
16	Wisdom	446	2151
17	Compassion	424	1472
18	Apostleship	346	1007
19	Interpretation of Tongues	65	203
20	Tongues	41	67
		18,258	58,718

TABLE 3

Laity Spiritual Giftedness (Sample Size N=17,234) ranked by Secondary Gift

		Primary Gift	Secondary Gift
1	Faith	1871	5908
2	Healing	1776	5544
3	Helping/Assistance	2160	5219
4	Teaching	1323	4000
5	Administration	1321	3749
6	Shepherding	1025	3699
7	Leadership	551	3497
8	Knowledge	1049	3484
9	Miracles	1343	3360
10	Servanthood	1040	2988
11	Giving	927	2872
12	Evangelism	522	2769
13	Exhortation	78	2606
14	Prophecy	606	2477
15	Wisdom	446	2151
16	Discernment	644	1646
17	Compassion	424	1472
18	Apostleship	346	1007
19	Interpretation of Tongues	65	203
20	Tongues	41	67
		18,258	58,718

TABLE 4

Clergy Spiritual Giftedness (Sample Size N=3,648) ranked by Primary Gift

		Primary Gift	Secondary Gift
1	Healing	317	853
2	Faith	296	1025
3	Teaching	289	1142
4	Knowledge	287	807
5	Servanthood	280	879
6	Shepherding	279	766
7	Helping/Assistance	269	729
8	Administration	259	594
9	Prophecy	229	896
	Miracles	229	845
11	Leadership	197	539
12	Exhortation	176	584
13	Evangelism	165	401
14	Giving	126	442
15	Wisdom	103	348
16	Compassion	101	409
17	Discernment	95	294
18	Apostleship	69	270
19	Interpretation of Tongues	6	34
20	Tongues	3	32
		3,775	11,889

TABLE 5

Clergy Spiritual Giftedness (Sample Size N=3,648) ranked by Secondary Gift

		Primary Gift	Secondary Gift
1	Teaching	289	1142
2	Faith	296	1025
3	Prophecy	229	896
4	Servanthood	280	879
5	Healing	317	853
6	Miracles	229	845
7	Knowledge	287	807
8	Shepherding	279	766
9	Helping/Assistance	269	729
10	Administration	259	594
11	Exhortation	176	584
12	Leadership	197	539
13	Giving	126	442
14	Compassion	101	409
15	Evangelism	165	401
16	Wisdom	103	348
17	Discernment	95	294
18	Apostleship	69	270
19	Interpretation of Tongues	6	34
20	Tongues	3	32
		3,775	11,889

TABLE 6

Youth Spiritual Giftedness (Sample Size N=988) ranked by Primary Gift

		Primary Gift	Secondary Gift
1	Servanthood	99	289
2	Leadership	85	264
3	Helping/Assistance	82	258
4	Shepherding	75	215
5	Compassion	72	264
6	Exhortation	66	207
7	Prophecy	64	176
8	Teaching	61	224
	Healing	61	183
10	Miracles	60	233
11	Faith	50	238
	Wisdom	50	110
13	Evangelism	41	133
14	Giving	40	153
15	Administration	38	70
16	Knowledge	36	148
17	Discernment	33	48
18	Apostleship	7	12
19	Tongues	5	7
20	Interpretation of Tongues	3	17
		1,028	3,249

TABLE 7

Youth Spiritual Giftedness (Sample Size N=988) ranked by Secondary Gift

		Primary Gift	Secondary Gift
1	Servanthood	99	289
2	Leadership	85	264
	Compassion	72	264
4	Helping/Assistance	82	258
5	Faith	50	238
6	Miracles	60	233
7	Teaching	61	224
8	Shepherding	75	215
9	Exhortation	66	207
10	Healing	61	183
11	Prophecy	64	176
12	Giving	40	153
13	Knowledge	36	148
14	Evangelism	41	133
15	Wisdom	50	110
16	Administration	38	70
17	Discernment	33	48
18	Interpretation of Tongues	3	17
19	Apostleship	7	12
20	Tongues	5	7
		1,028	3,249

TABLE 8

151

District Superintendent Spiritual Giftedness (Sample Size N=59) by Primary Gift

		Primary Gift	Secondary Gift
1	Administration	19	30
2	Faith	12	44
3	Teaching	9	14
4	Knowledge	6	18
5	Healing	3	16
	Servanthood	3	8
7	Leadership	2	9
	Prophecy	2	5
	Exhortation	2	3
10	Shepherding	1	9
	Miracles	1	7
	Evangelism	1	5
	Compassion	1	2
14	Helping/Assistance	0	8
	Giving	0	5
	Wisdom	0	3
	Discernment	0	1
	Apostleship	0	1
	Tongues	0	0
	Interpretation of Tongues	0	0
		62	188

TABLE 9

District Superintendent Spiritual Giftedness (Sample Size N=59) by Secondary Gift

		Primary Gift	Secondary Gift
1	Faith	12	44
2	Administration	19	30
3	Knowledge	6	18
4	Healing	3	16
5	Teaching	9	14
6	Leadership	2	9
	Shepherding	1	9
8	Servanthood	3	8
	Helping/Assistance	0	8
10	Miracles	1	7
11	Prophecy	2	5
	Evangelism	1	5
	Giving	0	5
14	Exhortation	2	3
	Wisdom	0	3
16	Compassion	1	2
17	Discernment	0	1
	Apostleship	0	1
19	Tongues	0	0
20	Interpretation of Tongues	0	0
		62	188

TABLE 10

Gender-Based Spiritual Giftedness—Male (Sample Size N=8,838) by Primary Gift

		Primary Gift	Secondary Gift
1	Healing	1005	2943
2	Helping/Assistance	874	1784
3	Administration	837	2172
4	Teaching	822	2314
5	Faith	802	2843
	Knowledge	802	2188
7	Shepherding	704	2277
8	Miracles	629	1388
9	Servanthood	462	1779
10	Giving	347	1326
11	Leadership	329	1534
12	Prophecy	326	1484
13	Evangelism	309	1110
14	Apostleship	295	651
15	Exhortation	258	1244
16	Wisdom	168	999
17	Discernment	163	737
18	Compassion	121	564
19	Interpretation of Tongues	25	95
20	Tongues	9	39
		9,287	29,471

TABLE 11

Gender-Based Spiritual Giftedness—Male (Sample Size N=8,838) by Secondary Gift

		Primary Gift	Secondary Gift
1	Healing	1005	2943
2	Faith	802	2843
3	Teaching	822	2314
4	Shepherding	704	2277
5	Knowledge	802	2188
6	Administration	837	2172
7	Helping/Assistance	874	1784
8	Servanthood	462	1779
9	Leadership	329	1534
10	Prophecy	326	1484
11	Miracles	629	1388
12	Giving	347	1326
13	Exhortation	258	1244
14	Evangelism	309	1110
15	Wisdom	168	999
16	Discernment	163	737
17	Apostleship	295	651
18	Compassion	121	564
19	Interpretation of Tongues	25	95
20	Tongues	9	39
		9,287	29,471

TABLE 12

Gender-Based Spiritual Giftedness—Female (Sample Size N=12,044) by Primary Gift

		Primary Gift	Secondary Gift
1	Helping/Assistance	1555	4164
2	Faith	1365	4090
3	Healing	1088	3454
4	Miracles	943	2817
5	Servanthood	858	2088
6	Teaching	790	2828
7	Administration	743	2171
8	Giving	706	1988
9	Exhortation	696	1946
10	Shepherding	600	2188
11	Discernment	576	1203
12	Knowledge	534	2103
13	Prophecy	509	1889
14	Leadership	419	2502
15	Compassion	404	1317
16	Wisdom	381	1500
17	Evangelism	378	2060
18	Apostleship	120	626
19	Interpretation of Tongues	46	142
20	Tongues	35	60
		12,746	41,136

TABLE 13

Gender-Based Spiritual Giftedness—Female (Sample Size N=12,044) by Secondary Gift

		Primary Gift	Secondary Gift
1	Helping/Assistance	1555	4164
2	Faith	1365	4090
3	Healing	1088	3454
4	Teaching	790	2828
5	Miracles	943	2817
6	Leadership	419	2502
7	Shepherding	600	2188
8	Administration	743	2171
9	Knowledge	534	2103
10	Servanthood	858	2088
11	Evangelism	378	2060
12	Giving	706	1988
13	Exhortation	696	1946
14	Prophecy	509	1889
15	Wisdom	381	1500
16	Compassion	404	1317
17	Discernment	576	1203
18	Apostleship	120	626
19	Interpretation of Tongues	46	142
20	Tongues	35	60
		12,746	41,136

TABLE 14

Comparative Primary Gifts Ranking by Jurisdiction
(representing 3,672 congregations and/or conferences)

	Northeast	Southeast	North Central	South Central	Western	Central Conferences
1	Faith	Faith	Healing	Faith	Healing	Faith
2	Teaching	Helping	Faith	Teaching	Shepherding	Healing
3	Administration	Healing	Helping	Healing	Faith	Miracles
4	Healing	Shepherding	Teaching	Helping	Helping	Prophecy
5	Helping	Miracles	Shepherding	Administration	Teaching	Wisdom
6	Knowledge	Teaching	Administration	Shepherding	Administration	Evangelism
7	Shepherding	Servanthood	Knowledge	Miracles	Knowledge	Shepherding
8	Miracles	Administration	Miracles	Servanthood	Miracles	Servanthood
9	Servanthood	Knowledge	Leadership	Knowledge	Servanthood	Compassion
10	Leadership	Exhortation	Giving	Giving	Prophecy	Helping
11	Prophecy	Giving	Prophecy	Prophecy	Leadership	Teaching
12	Exhortation	Leadership	Servanthood	Exhortation	Giving	Leadership
13	Wisdom	Prophecy	Exhortation	Leadership	Discernment	Giving
14	Evangelism	Evangelism	Evangelism	Evangelism	Compassion	Exhortation
15	Discernment	Wisdom	Compassion	Compassion	Exhortation	Knowledge
16	Giving	Discernment	Wisdom	Discernment	Apostleship	Interpretation
17	Compassion	Compassion	Discernment	Wisdom	Wisdom	Discernment
18	Apostleship	Apostleship	Apostleship	Apostleship	Evangelism	Tongues
19	Interpretation	Interpretation	Interpretation	Interpretation	Interpretation	Administration
20	Tongues	Tongues	Tongues	Tongues	Tongues	Apostleship
	N=891	N=801	N=571	N=718	N=593	N=98

TABLE 15

Comparative Primary Gifts —
The United Methodist Church and Other Denominational or Secular Groups

	UMC	Carmelite/ Benedictine	Assemblies Of God	Presbyterian	University Administrators	Nurses/ Health Care
1	Helping	Faith	Helping	Helping	Teaching	Healing
2	Faith	Wisdom	Evangelism	Teaching	Administration	Compassion
3	Healing	Miracles	Faith	Faith	Knowledge	Miracles
4	Teaching	Healing	Administration	Administration	Shepherding	Faith
5	Administration	Discernment	Miracles	Knowledge	Servanthood	Servanthood
6	Miracles	Compassion	Giving	Healing	Wisdom	Discernment
7	Knowledge	Helping	Healing	Shepherding	Prophecy	Administration
8	Servanthood	Shepherding	Leadership	Miracles	Leadership	Giving
9	Shepherding	Knowledge	Apostleship	Servanthood	Giving	Teaching
10	Giving	Servanthood	Exhortation	Leadership	Discernment	Knowledge
11	Exhortation	Giving	Teaching	Giving	Compassion	Wisdom
12	Prophecy	Administration	Shepherding	Compassion	Exhortation	Helping
13	Leadership	Leadership	Servanthood	Discernment	Healing	Exhortation
14	Discernment	Teaching	Tongues	Wisdom	Helping	Evangelism
15	Evangelism	Prophecy	Interpretation	Exhortation	Miracles	Shepherding
16	Wisdom	Exhortation	Knowledge	Prophecy	Faith	Leadership
17	Compassion	Evangelism	Prophecy	Evangelism	Interpretation	Prophecy
18	Apostleship	Apostleship	Wisdom	Apostleship	Tongues	Interpretation
19	Interpretation	Interpretation	Discernment	Interpretation	Evangelism	Tongues
20	Tongues	Tongues	Compassion	Tongues	Apostleship	Apostleship

TABLE 16

"The Next Best Thing to Jesus Christ"
Dialogue Sermon by Barbara Miller & Dan Dick
February 21, 1999, for Towson United Methodist Church in Towson, MD

Barbara (*from lectern or pulpit*): "Now you are the body of Christ, and individually members of it. Just as the body is one and has many members, and all the members of the body, though many, are one body, so it is with Christ." Christ is the head of the body, but sometimes it is easy to forget that fact.

(*Dan and Barbara move to center of chancel.*)

Dan: Hello, are you Barbara Miller?
Barbara: Yes, I'm the P.P.R.C. chair, and you must be Reverend Dick.
Dan: Please, call me Dan.
Barbara: Oh, Reverend Dick, you don't know how excited we are to meet you. We've been waiting a long time for this. Don't get me wrong, we love our pastor, but we've just worn him to a frazzle. We need some new blood.
Dan: Really? Well, I must say that I'm full of energy and ideas. The district superintendent told me that this was a real opportunity. I hope we like each other.
Barbara: I'm sure we will. We're a friendly church. You'll love us, Reverend Dick.
Dan: Dan, call me Dan. Can you tell me a little about the church? About what you're looking for from a pastor?
Barbara: Oh, this is a wonderful church. We have so many things going on. We have three worship services each week!
Dan: Three services, wow. I'll bet that involves a lot of the laity in leading worship.
Barbara: Oh, not really. Our pastor is so good. He preaches at all three services, and he mostly leads the services.
Dan: That's a lot of work, designing three services every week.
Barbara: Well, it's really the same service that we do three times. Our choir doesn't want to learn too much music, and the pastor says he can't write more than one sermon each week. We do have a keyboard—and sometimes even drums—at the middle service!
Dan: That's great. Do you attract a lot of young people?
Barbara: You know, that's a funny thing. We jazzed up the music at our middle service, but for some reason we haven't gotten any young people out. Reverend Dick, it's just a mystery.
Dan: What kind of education opportunities do you have?
Barbara: We have a super Sunday school program. We have something for all ages of children. The classes aren't large, but our teachers are so committed—most of them have been at it for forty years.

Dan: What about classes for adults?

Barbara: We have a hard time getting adults interested. Since the pastor is in all three worship services, he doesn't have time to teach a class, so we have coffee fellowship instead.

Dan: So there are no adult classes?!

Barbara: Well, we do have classes, Reverend Dick, where we discuss topics and what's going on in our lives. We do have a DISCIPLE class that meets Wednesday evenings. The pastor teaches that.

Dan: Why don't other adults lead the classes?

Barbara: Well, you know, we're experienced enough to teach the children, but we're not qualified to teach the Bible to other adults. Our pastor sets a really high standard—everyone's afraid they won't measure up. He is so good!

Dan: Well, that's nice, but it's a shame more people don't experience the joy of teaching. What special ministries do you have?

Barbara: Oh, we have some wonderful ministries! Our pastor takes a group of us to work at the soup kitchen downtown once a week, and sometimes we go to do hospital visits with him, and we've become quite well known in town for our counseling ministry—our pastor is a wonderful counselor. He also started a prayer group, and on the second Sunday evening of each month he conducts a healing service. It's kind of sad, though—he had to drop out of the choir when the healing services started. But, as you can see, our church is very active and has some great programs.

Dan: Is there anything you do that the pastor isn't involved in?

Barbara: No!! Isn't that amazing? He is such a fine role model—so faithful. He comes to every meeting, all our fellowship events—he even sets up tables before and sweeps the floor after! We all feel very comfortable and free to call him any time of the day or night. He's wonderful. If only…

Dan: If only what??

Barbara: Well, he already does so much.…

Dan: But?

Barbara: Well, what we would really love is a pastor who would visit. Our church has seven hundred families in it, and we figure that if he'd only do five visits a day, he could cover the entire congregation in less than half a year!

Dan: I see. Well, doesn't anyone else do visitation?

Barbara: Oh, sure they do, but there is nothing like a visit from the pastor. People seem to like that a lot more. He's so good in so many ways—if he could only complete the package by improving his visiting.

Dan: It sounds like you want Jesus himself.

Barbara (*laughing*)**:** That's funny, Reverend Dick. Our pastor is very good, but no, he's not Jesus. We think of him as the next best thing to Jesus Christ.

Dan: It sounds like very big shoes to fill. How long has he been here?

Barbara: Just under a year.

Dan *(looking at his watch)*: Oh, you know what? If you could direct me to a telephone—I need to call the district superintendent.…

(*Dan and Barbara move back to pulpit/lectern.*)

Barbara: "Indeed, the body does not consist of one member, but of many. The foot cannot say, 'Because I am not a hand, I am not a part of the body.' And the eye cannot say, 'Because I am not an ear, I am not a part of the body.' "

Dan: And as importantly, no eye should ever say, "Because you do not all see, you are worthless"; and it makes no sense to say that the body exists to fulfill only one function.

(*Dan and Barbara pull out telephone handsets.*)

Barbara: Hello, district superintendent's office. May I help you?

Dan: Uh, yeah, I think so. This is Dan Dick.

Barbara: Oh, hi Dan, it's me. Say, aren't you supposed to be interviewing with a church this evening?

Dan: Actually, that's where I'm calling from. I wanted to check with you to make sure that there hasn't been … um, some kind of mistake.

Barbara: What do you mean?

Dan: Well, as I recall, you asked me to consider this move because it was "a unique opportunity for me to fully utilize my gifts for ministry in a church that was about ready to take off." I think those are your exact words —and I'm not sure I'm in the right place.

Barbara: Why's that?

Dan: Well, I've met with a number of people here and they all seem perfectly content to be ministered to, but no one seems to think that the ministry is to be performed by anyone but the pastor.

Barbara: I told you it was a unique opportunity.

Dan: Can I just ask you—why me? Why here?

Barbara: Dan, you've been a very capable pastor. Your churches are extremely stable; you're a good shepherd; and your congregations always pay their apportionments in full. Towson Church is a bigger church, with lots of good people, and I think you can help them with their stewardship.

Dan: You mean, help them pay their apportionments?

Barbara: Certainly not just that—though that's a fine place to start. Just get in there, roll up your sleeves, and grow that church. There is growth in the area, you have a strong base—there's no reason not to succeed.

159

Dan: Well, why not send someone with gifts in evangelism or servanthood or leadership? You know my gifts are wisdom and discernment, and I'm not big on administration or outreach. This church needs someone to really lead them outside themselves.

Barbara: Nonsense! You're as good as anyone else. You'll do fine. Don't get so hung up on your gifts—you'll use them plenty, and others, too. If you're not strong in administration and outreach—what better place to learn?

Dan: Don't you think it would be better to match the gifts of the pastor with the specific needs of the congregation?

Barbara: We've matched your gifts, but also your years of service, your background, and your ability to get things done. Trust me—you are the best person for this appointment. You'll do fine.

Dan: What happens if I don't accept this appointment?

Barbara: That will put us in a very awkward position. We really went out on a limb here. We played you up as "the next best thing to Jesus Christ." We will give you another interview, but the options are limited. I need to tell you that the cabinet will be *very* disappointed if you turn down this opportunity.

Dan: I want to take time to pray about this, but I really don't think it is in my best interest, or more especially in the best interest of this church to put me here—after all, discernment and wisdom are my gifts.

Barbara: Right. Well, okay. I'll be in touch.

Dan: Bye.

(*Putting phones away*)

Barbara: "But each of us was given grace according to the measure of Christ's gift. The gifts he gave were that some would be apostles, some prophets, and some evangelists."

Dan: "Some will be pastors and teachers, some helpers and administrators, some leaders and some servants." Each gift is needed, no one person will possess them all.

Barbara: These gifts are given "for building up the body of Christ, until all of us come to the unity of the faith and of the knowledge of the Son of God, to maturity, to the measure of the full stature of Christ."

Dan: "But speaking the truth in love, we must grow up in every way into him who is the head, into Christ, from whom the whole body, joined and knit together by every ligament with which it is equipped, as each part is working properly, promotes the body's growth in building itself up in love."

(*Dan and Barbara move to the center of the chancel.*)

Barbara: Hi, I'm Barbara Miller, the lay leader here.

Dan: Um, I'm Dan Dick. You know, it's funny, but I met someone named Barbara Miller at my last interview.

Barbara: Isn't that odd?

Dan: A little, but you're nothing like her. You do remind me of my district superintendent, though.

Barbara: She must be a wonderful person! I wanted to take some time to sit with you before we meet with the Pastor-Parish Relations Committee.

Dan: I really appreciate that. I find that I can get to know a church better talking one-on-one with people than I can in a formal interview.

Barbara: There are a few things I think you should know about us before you meet with the committee.

Dan: Anything I should be worried about?

Barbara: Oh, no, but we've been told before that we're not like other churches, and there's some fear that you might come in and try to change things.

Dan: People here are afraid of change?

Barbara: Not at all, but we have a definite sense of the kind of change we're interested in. This congregation has a real sense of call, a vision of what God most wants us to do. We want a pastor to help keep us focused, not tell us what to do.

Dan: I see. What exactly is the role of the pastor here?

Barbara: There is no "role," per se. We can't tell you what we expect from you until we know what you're good at—what your gifts and passions are. Our current pastor is a wonderful healer and shepherd. She's helped us be much more nurturing and loving than before—but that was her—she taught us to do many of the things she did. You? You'll be different.

Dan: You don't see me "filling her shoes"?

Barbara: Not unless you are good at what she was good at. By the way, what do you think you're good at?

Dan: Well, others tell me that I am extremely insightful, creative, and energetic. I love to teach and preach, but I must admit that I'm a nightmare at administration and organization.

Barbara: That won't be a problem here. We're very organized. We have a lot of gifted people who work together well. Your focus on education and worship is a good fit. Those are areas where we want to improve. Now, we really don't have a lot of people who know how to do evangelism and outreach, but that hasn't been a problem so far. Our church has become a real community center, and our growth is due primarily to the fact that we do what we're good at and we don't try to do what we aren't good at.

Dan: Um, you're not expecting your new pastor to do all the things your congregation isn't good at, are you?

Barbara: Why would we? The pastor is just one member of the church like everybody else. How fair would it be for us to expect you, or anyone, to be good at everything? That's unreasonable.

Dan: I can't tell you how glad I am to hear you say that. What are the education ministries like here?

Barbara: We have a variety of experiences for all ages. We don't have a traditional Sunday school program—new short-term classes and programs begin and end on a regular basis. Most people—children included—are in new learning experiences every few months or so.

Dan: What would the church expect from me as a teacher?

Barbara: We tend to talk more about "leading learning opportunities" than about teaching. While I'm sure you have interesting things to say, we need to learn how to learn more than we need to be taught, in the traditional sense. It is more important to us that you come as a fellow learner than as a teacher.

Dan: What a wonderful concept. It will give me a lot more time to focus on preaching and attending meetings.

Barbara: Um, what meetings are you specifically referring to? In this church we only attend meetings in which we are directly involved. We're organized in teams of five to seven people, and usually the pastor isn't involved. The only meetings our pastor goes to are the ones where she's invited.

Dan: You mean the pastor isn't expected to go to all the different meetings?

Barbara: That would be a waste of time. The way we see it, you are a specially trained leadership resource for this congregation. We want to put you to maximum use. Wasting your time wastes our time and money. We need you to help us do the ministry effectively, faithfully, and appropriately.

Dan: Wow, it sounds like I wouldn't have to worry about much more than leading worship and preaching.

Barbara: Well, about that. We strongly believe that worship isn't something that we passively receive, but something we actively engage in. We have a lay preachers guild in this church. So far seventy-three people are in it. Membership in the guild requires that a person preach twice here and once at another church or public event. We have two Sunday services and a Saturday service, and there are actually weeks where the pastor doesn't preach even once. We also involve about a dozen people in designing and leading each worship experience.

Dan: I guess I'll need to spend time out in the community, just to have something to do.

Barbara: You won't be doing that alone, either. We have an active visitation program where we cluster newcomers with longer-term members. Right now, we have fifty-five cells. Each cell is made up of about a dozen people—active and inactive alike. Every six months we, as a church, covenant together to keep an eye on each other and check in from time to time. We were careful to make sure that each cell has people with caring gifts of healing, compassion, shepherding, and helping. It has made us very connected. We drop in on one another—or just make a call or drop a card in the mail—all the time.

Dan: That's amazing. So what exactly would I do here? It sounds like you're designed to get along just fine without a pastor.

Barbara: Oh, no. We need a pastoral leader to keep the whole system in view—to see where we're effective and where we need help. To help us examine our gifts and our vision. To encourage us to grow. We need a leader who will nurture us in our gifts. We need the theological expertise and training of an ordained leader. What we don't need is someone to tell us what to do—we need someone who will enable us to discover who we are. We don't want to know what you think we should be doing, we want to know what God thinks we should be doing.

Dan: I would welcome the opportunity to learn to be that kind of pastor.

Barbara: We pride ourselves on being "pastor-proof."

Dan: What do you mean by that?

Barbara: I mean that our church benefits from the pastor but isn't dependent on the pastor for success or failure. Not too long ago, every time we changed pastors it was like starting over again. Then, we realized that being the church means never depending on any one human being for purpose and direction. We need to be faithful and strong regardless of who is appointed as our pastor. When our church depended on the pastor for effectiveness, we were failing in many ways. When we finally understood what it means to be—truly be—the body of Christ, we understood that the whole reason for being here was to become the next best thing to Jesus Christ.

(Dan and Barbara move back to pulpit/lectern.)

Dan: The apostle Paul held a vision for the church—the body of Christ built upon the gifts that God gives through the Holy Spirit. This vision offered no distinction between clergy and laity, no division between men and women, no conflict between young and old. All people fit together to form the body; all gifts knit together to be the church. Designed and empowered this way, the church is not the next best thing to Jesus Christ, but it is Jesus Christ—incarnate and active in our world.

Barbara: Who we are is not dependent upon what we do. What we do reflects who we are, whose we are, and the will of the one who created us. Let us seek God's blessing that we might be the body of Christ—gifted, graced, and ready to serve a world that deeply needs to know the love of God. Let us pray…

SERMON REFLECTION GUIDE
"The Next Best Thing to Jesus Christ"

February 21, 1999

In this morning's sermon, the focus is on what it means to be the body of Christ—the church defined by the spiritual gifts and ministry passions of the members of the congregation.

Some terms used in the sermon may be unfamiliar. To assist newcomers to The United Methodist Church, and as a quick reminder for others, here are some brief definitions of the terms, a few Scripture passages with a related focus, and three personal reflection questions. We encourage you to share your reflections with friends, family members, or others from the church.

P.P.R.C.—the Pastor-Parish Relations Committee (or Staff-Parish Relations Committee) in United Methodist churches works with the district superintendent and bishop in securing clergy leadership for the church. This consultation and advisory function sometimes may include interviews with potential new pastors. The committee also monitors the ongoing relationship of the pastor and staff to the ministry of the congregation.

District Superintendent—a regional official who serves as principal administrator and as "pastor to pastors" within designated districts.

Apportionments—the money that each congregation of The United Methodist Church provides to the denomination to pay for structural, missional, programmatic, and staff costs.

Gifts—the spiritual gifts, as designated in the writings ascribed to the apostle Paul, that are given to each person through God's Holy Spirit for the building of the body of Christ.

Lay Leader—an elected member of each congregation who works in partnership with the appointed pastor(s) in the local church. Lay leaders provide a critical ministry of service, support, and leadership to the congregation.

Team—"a small number of people with complementary skills who are committed to a common purpose, performance goals, and approach for which they hold themselves mutually accountable."[1]

Cells—small groups designed to help people practice the means of grace and join together in meaningful Christian community.

Four Scripture Passages for Reading and Reflection
1 Corinthians 12:1-31 (and read 1 Corinthians chapter 13, reflecting on how these
    familiar words of love fulfill Paul's promise that they are "a more excellent way")
Romans 12:1-8
Ephesians 4:7-16
1 Peter 4:10

Reflection Questions: Please take some time to reflect on these three questions. You
will benefit greatly from talking with another person about both the questions and your
reflections.

1. What does it mean to be a member of the body of Christ? What are
   the benefits and the costs of such membership?
2. What does it mean to be a minister of the gospel of Jesus Christ?
   What are the ministries to which God calls people beyond the institution of "the church"?
3. Christian stewardship is the wise management and employment of
   everything we have been given by God. If we are to be good and faithful stewards of the gifts God has given us, what assistance and guidance
   do we need in order to do so?

NOTES

1. Reprinted by permission of Harvard Business School Press. From *The Wisdom of Teams* by Jon
   R. Katzenbach and Douglas K. Smith. Boston, MA 1993, p. 45. Copyright © 1993 by
   McKinsey & Company, Inc. All rights reserved.